$2-

Make it an Adventure

Books by Marcus Bach

Strange Altars

The Dream Gate

Major Religions of the World

The Will to Believe

Report to Protestants

God and the Soviets

Faith and My Friends

Adventures in Faith

He Talked with God

The Circle of Faith

Of Faith and Learning

They Have Found a Faith

Strange Sects and Curious Cults

Had You Been Born in Another Faith

The Unity Way of Life

Make it an Adventure

MARCUS BACH

PRENTICE-HALL, INC.
Englewood Cliffs, N.J.

To my friend
Shirley H. Mitchell
who made it an adventure
in the field of American transportation

CONTENTS

Make it an Adventure

PART ONE

The Personal Adventure

1

Something to live by

I found it in many lands. I heard it in many languages. But the meaning was always the same: *The greatest secret of living is to make life an adventure!*

Here was one belief which every culture and every people agreed upon. Here was one technique which everyone could use regardless of where he lived, and when I learned it I understood for the first time why some people get the most out of life and others do not.

Here was the secret spark that spelled the difference between greatness and littleness, between success and failure, between a zest for living and a dull, dreary outlook on life.

Make it an adventure!

I had no idea how quickly I would be called upon to test the power of these words in my own experience and to prove whether or not they actually worked for me.

There Was Voodoo

I had gone to the West Indies to get a story on the mystery and magic of Haitian Voodoo. Forbidden Voodoo. Voodoo on the plains of Leogane and in the hill country near Jacmel, a half-deserted city on the sea. I had been warned not to go by a psychic-minded friend who said, "Voodoo is black magic and witchcraft. Don't go to Haiti."

But I went. Then one morning, January 6, I got up only to stagger groggily back into bed. Soon a feverish mist closed in, accompanied by stabbing pains in my solar plexus. My wife stuck a fever thermometer into my mouth. Through moist eyes I saw her horrified expression.

Because we had no telephone in our modest room at the Hotel Excelsior in Port-au-Prince, after one quick glance at the thermometer reading, Lorena rushed down to the lobby to call a doctor. I tried hazily to figure out what had happened, reminding myself that for days I had been dragging myself around. As I lay there consoling myself that it was nothing serious, I heard the door open slowly.

Raising myself with effort, I saw Ariette, the maid, cautiously peering in. Her face was a haunting black against the white door. Her eyes were wide with frightened concern.

"You *seeck?*" she asked.

I nodded. Yes, I was sick.

She was in the room now with a hand on the doorknob. Standing on tiptoe to see me better, she said a single word, "*Wanga!*" That was to say, "Who put a hex on you!"

"*Wanga?*" I repeated weakly and heard the door close.

It was a bad word, a disturbing word. *Wanga* meant a bad luck charm used by unscrupulous Voodoo priests to psychologically attack their victims. In a blurred vision, I recalled a black Voodoo doll, a *wanga,* which a *houngan* (Voodoo priest) had shown me in his private chapel. Then the warning came flooding in, "Don't go to Haiti!" Scenes of Voodoo ceremonies flashed like burning torches in my mind. Sounds of Voodoo chants pounded through my thoughts. I remembered how Lorena had taken pictures of Voodoo rituals on the sly. I recalled that I had been warned about staying away from a certain peristyle, a Voodoo meeting place, but we had gone just the same. Remembering these things, I got sicker and sicker.

The doctor, a German named Carl Wilhelm Lembke, came in; he was a loveable, talented doctor who had been in Haiti for thirty years. He was not sure about *wangas*, but he was sure about malaria, and he brushed aside my idiosyncrasies about pill-taking and shots and forced me to accept medical skill. Malaria and a hundred-and-four-degree fever would not let me resist.

But it was not only malaria. It was fear. *Wanga* fear. Also the fear of a prolonged confinement, fear of what I had read about the recurrence of malaria, fear about what was happening to my busy schedule, fear about my work, fear about my career. Restlessly I tossed. Deliriously I dreamed. Impatiently I fought against the imposition of this set-back, wondering why that one mosquito packing that malaria germ had singled me out somewhere in a swamp in Voodoo land.

Days were marked by the endless honking of horns, the cries of the vendors, the tap of the bootblack's box. Nights brought the barking of dogs, the murmur of distant drums, and the crowing of cocks in the moonlight. I had always thought I was a calm man, a man who could take it; but I needed something beyond the selfless care of Lorena and the pills and shots of Dr. Lembke.

I needed something tangible in the way of a philosophy. Shall we call it faith? Faith, too, I always felt I had. It is easy to talk about faith when things are going well, and when a man is feeling well, and when his world is well. I had often sat at bedsides and consoled people. I used to say to others, "Everything will be all right. Just have faith. Life moves in cycles, you know." I had all sorts of phrases and I believed them, too, or thought I did. It is different, however, when the room is swinging and you feel a two-ton weight on your solar plexus!

Then it dawned on me. Like a pinpoint of light. No bigger at first than that. A pinpoint of light in a dark and troubled sky. Then it grew. Steadily, surely, it grew as if it were the bearer of a message, clearing its way as it came, blazing its way with an ever-increasing brightness. Straight on down it came, as if it were heaven-sent.

I have no doubt it was. It *was* a message, one that I had learned in many lands and heard in many languages. It said,

"You came here to investigate the beliefs of others? What about your belief? You wanted to find out what others live by? What do *you* live by? You prided yourself on your courage at the Voodoo experiencies. What about *this* experience? You came to make your research here an adventure. Now things have changed and something unexpected and unforeseen has happened to you. *Make this* your adventure! For unless you meet life adventurously, you are lost indeed!"

It was that clear. It was that real. And the result was that phenomenal.

Make It an Adventure!

I lay there looking up at the monotonous ceiling and it suddenly did not seem monotonous any more. There was something in my mind that transformed it and romanticized it and filled the common, ordinary room with hope. It was the affirmation contained in the four remarkable words, "Make it an adventure!"

Dr. Lembke became not only a figure and a form, but a friend. Ariette, the maid, whose *wanga* talk had been so disturbing, suddenly became a challenge for me and when next she came in I managed to say, "There may be *wangas*, Ariette, but there are also *paquets*. You know what *paquets* are? They are good luck charms. If a man has a *paquet* that is stronger than the *wanga*, he need never fear the *wanga!* Didn't you know that?"

And Lorena said, "I don't know what has happened to you, but suddenly everything seems bright."

The Power of the Paquet

For a long time after I recovered and returned to the States I called the phrase, "Make It An Adventure," my *paquet*, my good luck charm. It was more than that. It was a belief, deep-seated and real, representing an attitude and a point of view which had power to help a man over life's rough spots. It was not a matter of faith in faith or belief in a belief; it was, rather, the conviction that we can win over obstacles if we have the will to win and that we can put affirmations to work at every point in life, especially an affirmation as strong as "Make It An Adventure."

Proofs of its strength were found in unexpected ways and in unexpected places. Once during a lecture assignment at the School of Mines in Rapid City, South Dakota, a very personable young man was waiting for me at the entrance of the auditorium. He stood on crutches and, introducing himself, said he merely wanted to add his welcome to my coming to the school. Since he was slightly beyond the average student age, I asked him whether he was on the teaching staff. He replied, "Yes, I am the wrestling coach."

My glance registered my surprise. The wrestling coach? The crutches, the paraplegic condition of the man, the disarming smile, left me with nothing more to say that, "Well, that's interesting!" A student bystander filled in by saying, "What's more, he's the best of coaches!"

With this, the wrestling coach said to me, "There is no reason why you should remember me, but several years ago you spoke at my high school graduation. In your talk you said we should make our life the great adventure. My ambition had always been to be a wrestler and when polio hit me I thought that everything was lost. Your 'Make It An Adventure' changed my mind. I began studying and reading all I could about wrestling. If I couldn't be a wrestler, the next best thing would be to train others through whom I could see myself wrestling. Thank you for helping me find my place in life."

I left the School of Mines with as great a blessing as can come to a speaker along his lecture route. Win or lose, this man who had found his "place in life" was beyond the shadow of doubt the "very best of coaches."

So great is a man's potential and so great, too, is the power of the *paquet!*

History Has Its Lessons

Historian Arnold J. Toynbee has an exciting observation in his *Study of History*. He presents the proposition that nations grow stronger in proportion to the difficulties encountered in their environment. Supporting this theory with the rise and fall of various cultures, he indicates with striking force that stimulus is continually needed if civilizations are not to end in obscurity. New frontiers, new struggles, new ground, the unexpected, the difficult, the challenging; these are not the killers but the makers of great nations. And what is true of nations is, of course, equally true of individuals, since a nation is but a family of persons living together with common aspirations and common concerns.

It is the individual we are talking about. *Make it an adventure* in your relationship with *yourself* is the subject of this section of our book. You are the key person and you are the most important figure in our discussion. But there is an interlocking relationship here between you and the nation in which you live. If we are continually urged to take the easy way, to spare ourselves, to no longer come to grips with the hard, cold ground of life, we are surely in danger of deteriorating.

"While a man should learn to pace himself," a doctor told me recently, "he should also learn not to pamper himself. During a recent snowstorm some of my colleagues made public statements to the effect that men over forty should shovel their walks only if they do it gently! And men over fifty should put their shovels away for good! I don't agree. That's pampering. Sure, there have been heart attacks due to shoveling snow, but there have also been heart attacks when men were driving their automobiles or playing golf. Should everyone over fifty put up his car or his golf clubs? Pace yourself. Approach your job with a spirit of fun. We scare too easily and some of us doctors help in the scaring process. One of the worst phrases we have is, 'Take it easy!' That is why we get soft. We ought to say, 'Take it hard!' Then we would get back to being strong men again!"

We *are* getting soft. We do not walk any more. In fact, many places now have perambulating sidewalks; all we need to do is step on. We do not climb stairs any more. New homes have eliminated stairs or have escalators to take their place. We do not push lawn-mowers any more; they now pull us. We do not even get up from our chairs to change TV programs. We do not even walk on the golf course any more. There is a promise that soon we will not even have to steer our automobiles.

If it is true that nations passed away in ancient times or that continents decayed or that religions died because they lost their cutting edge, then we had better take a long, hard look at ourselves! Someone may have put a *wanga* on us! But the *paquet* that can *"un-wanga"* us and change our attitude toward life is to MAKE IT AN ADVENTURE.

And Many Do Make It an Adventure!

Every once in a while in my research I meet individuals who have a plus factor of pep. I used to wonder what it was that gave them this extra zest. Vitamins? Miracle drugs? Money? Surely it must be something profound, I thought, whatever it is. I learned it was something so remarkably simple that the average person was reluctant to take it seriously—until he found it for himself.

A buoyantly healthy man in India explained it to me this way, "We must teach people in the West how to *breathe*. With all their wealth and ingenuity, they still have not found the greatest treasure: *Pranayama!*

The word was not nearly as difficult as it sounded. In Sanskrit *Prana* means breath and *Yama* means a pause. In other words, *Pranayama* is controlled breathing, conscious breathing, breathing with a purpose. *Pranayama* has nothing to do with medication or shots. It has nothing to do with fadism. It has to do with air. A-I-R. Fresh air and breathing.

The secret of *Pranayama* is this: breathing has a "spiritual cosmic content" and awakens a subtle psychic force within you. You can test it for yourself. Right now, take a deep, relaxed inhalation to the count of four, rest for four counts, then exhale for four counts. Do this unhurriedly four times. Notice how conducive this is to releasing tension. Observe how much more erect you are sitting, how much straighter your spine, how improved your sense of well-being appears to be. And you have spent approximately two minutes out of your twenty-four hour day! *Two minutes* and something has already happened to you!

Imagine what would happen (or try it for yourself) if you were to go to the open window or outside in the fresh air and spend just two minutes more with this same immensely simple exercise. Or, try a short walk, consciously, rhythmically breathing with the same deep sense of awareness of *Pranayama*. When you do, when you realize what this elementary exercise does for you, you will say, "Why in the world don't I do this oftener and longer and develop it more?" You can. All you need to do is to make breathing an adventure.

I know many *swamis* and *yogis*. I recently wrote the preface for *The Complete Book of Yoga*, the famous work by Swami Vishnudevananda. All of my yogi friends tell me that the greatest secret in life is *Pranayama*. It is a deep and profound subject, but the gist of it is that every cell in one's body is controlled by "vital air" (*Prana*) and that harmonized breathing helps in the regulation and steadiness of body and mind.

One of the healthiest men I know claims that this is his secret technique for keeping well. He does not talk about it and I do not suppose he would ever have told me had it not been that I stepped out of his home with him one day. He paused and inhaled deeply of the crisp, autumn air. After he had exhaled very slowly and with control, he said, "Never step out of doors without taking a deep breath. It's the best therapy." For nearly eighteen years, ever since he was thirty, this businessman has started each day with a ten-minute breathing exercise. Frequently during the day when he is on the job, when he walks, when he relaxes, he breathes rhythmically, consciously. This is his secret and it is so simple that few will try it. But those who do try it learn what profound wonders it performs.

Literally, all we need to do to stay alive is to keep breathing! And all we need to do to breathe properly is to MAKE IT AN ADVENTURE.

No one can put a *wanga* on you, but if you insist, they can; remember, you can put a *paquet* on the *wanga* and defeat it.

Thoughts, as the saying goes, are things, but you can control them. This may require work, it may not always be easy, but it can be done even if you are lying in a sick room gazing at the ceiling, hearing the haunting throb of Voodoo drums.

A wrestling coach has proved that you can be what you wish to be. A doctor has told you that you can pace yourself and face yourself. A historian has advised us that challenges may be exactly what we need to bring out a new and greater strength within ourselves.

Here, then, is more than just a phrase. Here is something to live by, especially if you will put this approach at the hub of life and remember that no matter what you are called upon to do, you can *Make It An Adventure.*

2

Work at your weakness

What is your greatest weakness? What one thing holds you back from being your best and doing your best? What would you like most to overcome? It is at exactly this point that the adventurous spirit can most effectively prove its worth. Like a welded chain, your point of weakness can become your point of greatest strength if you will but work at it adventurously.

My files are full of proof of this. There was, for example, a woman in southern California. She was an artist. Not a great artist. In fact, a very frustrated one. She had had such a series of bad breaks that a year before I met her she was having trouble with her eyes and worrying that she might never be able to paint again. Her greatest weakness was expressed in her lament that, "Life has lost its joy."

She did not want life to lose its joy, but the more she tried to fight back, the more frustrated she became. Then she heard someone say, "If you want to remake your life a certain way, start living as though it was already remade. When you do that you will discover that a power within you is working with you."

Half in despair and half in hope, she said, "If this is true, I'm going to begin acting as though I were happy and radiant and bubbling over with joy."

12

But how to do this?

She went to the mirror and looked at herself and what she saw was far from joyful.

"I think," she told me, "I had been despondent and hopeless for so long that when I tried to smile, the mirror showed little more than a snarl. It was actually physically painful for me to smile, but I started. I kept at it. I stood in front of the mirror for a few minutes every day and forced myself to be happy and smile. Then I discovered that there *was* something deep in my soul that was coming to my aid. Every day it became more real, every day it became easier. Now people say to me, 'How do you get this radiance?' I know how I got it. I put it there. 'How is it that your eyes are better?' they want to know. 'It wasn't my eyes. It was me. I changed my life by sheer effort and by the determination to be what I wanted to be.'"

In short, she made it an adventure.

The logical question, of course, is, "What else can a person do? What is the alternative?"

There is no alternative unless you wish to become panicky, lose your sense of direction and balance, and thereby forfeit your best judgment in the matter. But even if you know your weakness and if you can analyze your trouble, it is often difficult to maintain a sense of calm. A psychiatrist confessed that even though he was able to help his patients with their problems, he was unable to help himself. He said, "When I saw my own troubles building up, I could recognize them and diagnose them, but I still did not know how to overcome them. They came toward me like a whirlwind and I seemed unable to hold them back."

That is a confession which many of us could also make. "Physician, heal thyself!" is a tormenting cry, but it is one which the spirit of adventure can ameliorate if we have the will to work at our weakness.

Every Situation
Is an Opportunity for Adventure

One day I came into Chicago's O'Hare airfield in a storm.
We landed on time and many of the passengers who had to
make close connections breathed a sigh of relief. Then as we
taxied slowly toward the terminal the captain announced that
we would have to wait thirty minutes for clearance because
of the heavy traffic and the weather. The thirty minutes
stretched into an hour, the hour into two hours, with no assurance of how long we would have to sit there listening to
the drone of the engines and gazing out at the steadily falling
snow on the windswept field.

It was interesting to note the reaction of the passengers as
the minutes dragged on into the third hour's wait. Some of
the people began arguing with the stewardesses. Others paced
up and down the aisle as if to infect everyone with their
annoyance. Being by nature impatient, I, too, could easily have
become upset at what seemed an intolerable delay. However,
"Make it an adventure" came to my rescue. "Work at your
weakness," something said to me, and I pulled a paperback
book out of my portfolio, one that I had been carrying with
me on many a trip but had never found time to read. After
all, it was a state of mind rather than a state of location in
which we were caught. Granted that connections would be
missed and that the tendency toward claustrophobia might be
great, what else was there to do but wait?

That period, those three hours and a half, was a classroom
period for me, teaching me the art of calm, instructing me
how to work at my weakness, reminding me of the need and
power of the adventurous life.

Air travel, becoming ever more popular, puts an added stress
on our already complicated culture. There is always a penalty
for every added luxury and a price we must pay for our lust
for convenience and speed. Anyone who has ever flown realizes
the ominous feeling of circling an airport while a fateful voice
over a microphone tells you, "It will be just a few moments,

folks!" All the while, even the most seasoned traveler wonders whether perhaps the landing gear has stuck or other mechanical trouble has occurred about which the helpless passengers are supposed to be kept in the dark.

But what is the alternative? Is there a better one than to sit back and make it an adventure?

Fatalism or Faith?

This may imply a blind acceptance of fate, but what is wrong with a good healthy fatalism? After all, there is in each of us a certain determinative factor which, whether we like it or not, whispers to us, "What will be, will be." There is nothing wrong with this unless it rules out fortitude to meet emergencies unless it makes us unwilling to use our capabilities in meeting and controlling situations. Faith is a mighty factor in this equation, and faith and fatalism are so closely interlaced that it is difficult to properly separate the two.

Hinduism has an interesting illustration in this connection. "Which is the greater," it asks, "the baby monkey clinging in confidence to its mother for protection, or the baby cat dangling from the firm grip of its mother's teeth as it is carried by the nape of its neck, confident that the mother will not let it fall?" Both the monkey and the cat, says the analogy, are manifesting faith in the mother according to their respective natures. One clings and the other is clung to. Fatalism or faith, it is an adventure either way.

Is it faith or fatalism to realize that there is always a greater person lurking within us than we ourselves customarily manifest? This sleeping giant, so-called, is aroused in many ways. Under proper circumstances a meek and submissive individual may suddenly become a courageous, fighting man. In the proper situation a burly, seemingly insensitive person may turn out to be a sentimentalist. There is a little of Dr. Jekyl and Mr. Hyde in everyone, and it is possible to call forth the best or the worst in us by our own command. The true adventurer, however, always calls forth the highest, for anything less than the best can hardly be called good sportsmanship, and the man who is absolutely sincere will try his best to work at his weakness.

Consider the AA's

For an example in how the adventurous life can remake individuals, consider the impressive work of Alcoholics Anonymous. This movement is one of the best examples of adventure at work and offers tangible evidence of the power of faith in the individual life. If you have ever tried to break a habit of long standing or to change a fixed pattern which has dominated you for years, you will appreciate the power of the Alcoholics Anonymous technique. Briefly stated, the alcoholic must recognize the need for his rehabilitation, must look for strength greater than any he has ever put to use, must fill every hour of his day with the adventurous spirit. Only then will it be possible for him to throw off his chains.

The word "Anonymous" is significant, for it indicates that the assignment is a personal one, whether the individual is great or small, known or unknown, rich or poor. Even the two founders of the AA are kept anonymous. They are referred to as simply Mr. Bill and Dr. Bob, drunkards, who surrendered their will to God and made their rehabilitation their great adventure.

By now the story has often been told of how Mr. Bill, though an avowed atheist, cried out, "If there be a God, let Him show Himself. I am ready to do anything." Suddenly in the hospital room where he lay he felt a Presence and saw what seemed to him a great light. Such was the beginning in 1934 of the movement which today has a membership of some 250,000 and is attracting about 25,000 new "converts" every year. It has an enviable record of 75% recovery from among those who will subscribe unreservedly to the four steps:

1. Have a genuine desire to be cured;
2. Admit that you cannot stop drinking by yourself;
3. Ask for God's help;
4. Accept and acknowledge this help.

Many an AA member has told me that when he realized his need to give up drinking, he began by saying to himself, "Now, God helping me, I will not touch the stuff for the next hour!" He actually timed himself and when the hour was up he repeated his affirmation for the next hour and then the next, on through the first day and into the night. It was a struggle and he knew it. It was an adventure, a case of life or death. The following day he repeated his hour-to-hour vigil again until he reached a point where he could say, "Now with God's help I will not touch the stuff throughout *the day*." Then with a twenty-four hour day conquered, he extended it to a number of days, then to a week and a month until God and he had mastered the problem.

It was not an experiment, not a matter of trial and error; it was an adventure in faith, an adventure in finding the power he needed and in using the power he found. He was aided in his adventure by others, and he helped himself by helping others who were in the same predicament as he, but most of all it was his own lonely project.

When the temptation was greatest, then his will had to be greatest, too, and when the desire to drink was highest, he had to adventure in a higher desire in which the lower desire could be sublimated. It was an adventure when he went to the AA meetings, when he testified about his experiences, when he met old friends who kidded him and reminded him of the "good old days." It was an adventure.

We Are All "Alcoholics" in a Way

Some of us are "alcoholics" when it comes to eating. The dubious question whether it is worse to be a drunkard than a glutton has been debated for a long time, but that the will power needed to overcome excessive eating is often as great as that needed to overcome excessive drinking has been rather well established.

We are just now slowly learning the truth of the adage, "You are what you eat." For the first time in history there

is a concerted effort to inform the public that our eating habits
generally are abominable, that we can be "well-fed" and still
be starving nutritionally and that we are living longer not
because of what we eat, but because science cajoles us into
our vaunted geriatric age through vitamins, antibiotics, food
supplements, miracle drugs and, all too infrequently, through
hints and secrets about exercise, diet, and health.

Dr. Thomas K. Cureton, director of physical fitness research,
says that our softness can best be overcome by hard physical
work and the addition of wheat germ and other nutritionally
high supplements in the diet. His studies show that athletics
in American life suffer from four major defects: young people
do not take physical fitness seriously during their high school
years nor do they compete in endurance events; they are care-
less or uninformed about diet in relation to performance; physical education is too emphatically a "fun course;" American
physicians discourage endurance work for American youth.

In this connection other researchers have pointed out that
our high school students average less than an hour a month in
physical education classes. In a rating of fitness tests, fifty-eight
percent of American youngsters failed one or more of the
tests, while less than nine percent of the European children
failed. British fitness in sports is twenty percent better than
is ours in the U.S.A.

All of this caused President Kennedy to say, "We are
becoming a nation of spectators," and prompted him to warn
that since we have lost the adventure of self participation in
sports, in health habits, and in the proper care of our bodies,
our nation is in danger of being weakened at the personal level.
Too many of us *are* content to sit on the sidelines and watch
others carry the ball, and about the only exercise some of us
get is by applauding those who are demonstrating the great
things that exercise can do.

The same thing is true about the way in which we meet our
emotional and other personal problems. Here, too, we find
symptoms closely paralleling alcoholism. We are afraid to be
alone and to face ourselves squarely, just as the alcoholic
drinks alone to keep himself from feeling alone; he refuses

to face himself as he knows he *is,* by changing himself into someone and something he is *not.* So people with emotional problems often look for sympathy and support for their weakness, hiding behind all sorts of excuses and trying to run from themselves.

Like the alcoholic, they will never effect a cure until they are ready to make their particular problem the great adventure.

Then There Is
the Will to Get Well

A young, ambitious doctor in the Kansas community where I was staying complained to the old hometown physician that he could not do a thing for Miss Amelia Fitch.

"I know it," the elder medic agreed. "Neither medicine nor religion has helped that old biddy. What someone ought to do is light a fire under her bed."

It worked. The young doctor lit a newspaper under the bed, shouted, "Fire!" and Miss Fitch has been on her feet ever since!

Other cases, more serious but just as self-centered, can be noted by the testimony of an arthritic sufferer who wrote me a forthright "confession."

"I was confined to my chair for three years," she related. "My knuckles were swollen and my right hand was clenched shut with stiffness. My neighbor said, 'Aren't you going to the big centennial celebration tomorrow? At one time you were one of the most important people in town.' I sighed and said, 'The spirit is willing, but the flesh is weak.' That was what I said, but did I really mean it? *Was* the spirit willing? Did I honestly want to go to the centennial celebration? I certainly did *not* want to go. That was the last thing I wanted to do. The chairman of the program committee was my bitterest enemy. She cut me out of the arrangements a long time ago with the announcement, 'She's always sick anyhow.' My family and my relatives made up for it. They gave me the pity I needed to compensate for the hurt I felt. It had been that way for years. For every selfish pity there were always those who justified me and for every emotional hurt there was a physical pain I could point to and which would help me get the care and affection I craved. I had lied to the neighbor. The spirit was *not* willing!"

There is something of the "miraculous" in this story, found not so much in the fact that this woman actually walked to the centennial celebration under her own power and that she extended an unclenched and unswollen hand to her "bitterest enemy;" the true miracle was that she succeeded in analyzing herself and in compelling her spirit to become *willing and adventurous.*

I asked her what triggered this sudden change.

"I just got to thinking," she said, "of how I really didn't want to be well and I decided to take the same effort and put it into the idea of *getting* well. Maybe it was selfishness all along the way. First I was selfish because I wanted pity and now I'm selfish because I want praise!"

Whatever it was, she worked at her weakness by making it an adventure!

So can I.

And so can you.

3

Always adventure

in your highest good

The spirit of adventure, as we are considering it, must always be in the area of your highest good. Obviously, swindlers and racketeers, no less than unscrupulous dictators, may feel they are leading adventurous lives. They may be, and so may cloak-and-dagger men and those who are "quick on the draw." Their emphasis, however, is faulty if it is not in accord with a recognition of their highest good. It is never truly adventurous to be less than your best.

There are others who may insist that the end justifies the means, but this, too, is not the kind of adventure we are talking about. Mankind has learned through a long history of trial and error that principles of virtue, goodness, justice, and right are qualities upon which humanity goes forward. And what is true of humanity is, of course, equally true of the individuals of which humanity consists. To shift the energy involved in doing wrong into a determination to do right constitutes one of the greatest adventures of all.

The classical example in this respect is Saul of Tarsus, the man who mobilized his energies with the avowed intention of persecuting the early Christians. Walking to Damascus to carry out these intentions, he had a vision and heard a voice which seemed to him to be the voice of God. God wanted to know what he was up to and asked, in effect, if that was the best that Saul could do with his life. Experiencing a conversion, Saul utilized the same pent-up energy for promoting, not persecuting, the Christian cause. His new name, Paul, gave further evidence of how complete and thorough the change in his life became.

The apostle Peter, too, has been cited as a man who made a choice when tormented by indecision as to the direction his life should take. Henryk Sienkiewicz wrote his great book, *Quo Vadis,* around this theme and described how Peter, turning his back upon his duty and his calling, was suddenly confronted by a vision of the Christ. Peter agonizingly asked just two words, "Quo vadis?" which is to say, "Where are you going?" and Christ replied, "To Rome to be crucified again." It was then that Peter found himself, rediscovered his highest good, and in the spirit of selfless adventure decided to go to Rome in the Master's place.

Every sincere changer-of-men seeks to work on this basis, causing us to ask ourselves, "Quo vadis?" Where are you going? Where should our life be invested? For the impulse toward doing good is constantly challenged by the impulse toward doing evil, but when we realize this we can use the tendency toward evil to make the tendency toward good more dynamic. Father Flanagan had this in mind when he said, "There is no such thing as a bad boy." He meant that the adventurous spirit, though often misguided, could be harnessed and channeled into constructive lives.

Our prisons are filled with men and women, and our juvenile homes are packed with young people who picked the wrong turning in the road. Every newspaper tells the ironic story of someone who needed advice and help along the way and who might have been as famous in the realm of constructive good as he became notorious in destructive evil. Paradoxically it would have been easier, too, and certainly much more profitable for them to have chosen the good.

Take the case of Mrs. Emma Geiger of Sheldon, Iowa, who was recently convicted as an embezzler in her father's bank. For years Mrs. Geiger kept two sets of books and lived two lives in the little midwestern community. The work and effort she put into this dual role took every moment of her time. She was never free from fear. She was never without her thoughts of guilt. She was constantly on the alert. She was never able to take a vacation. She was a genius in crime until she was caught, and with the same ingenuity she could have been a genius in constructive good.

In Indiana a thief admitted he worked for two months plotting the holdup of a supermarket. He familiarized himself with the work schedules of the employees. He knew every foot of the store and the premises. He had a perfect check on the patrolmen and knew almost to the minute where their prowl cars were at any given time. For sixty days and sixty nights he lived with the idea of the perfect crime in mind and worked out every detail like a general planning a campaign. He overlooked one fateful detail. At the moment of his holdup there happened to be a plainclothesman in the store buying a carton of cigarettes. This detective also happened to be armed and he shot the thief in the leg as he was making his getaway. In sentencing the holdup man the judge said, "Did you ever think of the money you might have made if you had worked at a legitimate job for the two months you spent in figuring out this 'perfect crime?' "

One day after I spoke to a group of inmates at a midwestern reformatory one of the young men sorrowfully told me that he thought his penalty of seven years had been too severe. All he did was drive the get-away car in the holdup of a storage firm. He waited at the wheel while two companions in the building rifled the safe. Apprehended by a watchman, the trio found that their night of crime had fizzled out.

"I wanted adventure," he told me, and he got it; but it was on the wrong level. That is the tragedy and that is the lament of many a potentially good person who, for the sake of kicks or thrills or out of sheer failure to think, adventures into darkness instead of light.

Strength Comes with the Doing

Each time a temptation is conquered or a weakness is overcome, you generate a greater resistance for meeting and conquering the next encounter. We build up a reservoir of strength as we exercise our will in these matters. Nature sharpens the will that is used and dulls the will that is abused.

Take the matter of fear, which is one psychosis we all must deal with somewhere along the way. It is generally conceded that fear can best be overcome by doing the thing which inspired the fear. Afraid of high places? Force yourself to take a plane ride or gather up your courage for a trip to the top of the Empire State Building. Afraid of the dark? Get yourself in hand and walk past the cemetery at night, even if you must whistle. If you are afraid of traveling, travel; afraid of the water, swim; afraid of people, begin being sociable. Do the thing you fear.

There is a chance that this can be carried too far. Caution may be a monitor warning us for our own good to be wary of just how far we should go or how much we are equipped to endure. But basically the injunction to do the thing you fear is sound and there is overwhelming evidence that the burden of truth is with the theorists. Within reason you can definitely conquer your misgivings and overcome your limitations by adventurously doing the things bounded by imaginary fears.

In my fledgling days as a public speaker I was a slave to the use of a manuscript during my talks. It was horrifying for me to think of speaking extemporaneously or to face an audience without the support of a well-prepared outline or a sheaf of notes. I greatly envied speakers who could get up and speak without a script, but I shuddered to think what would happen to me if I ever tried it. Nonetheless I decided to try and began by speaking off the cuff to imaginary audiences. All the while I was fearing the day when the empty benches would be filled with live and listening people.

But the day came and I not only made it an adventure, I made it the turning point in my relationship with audiences.

I remember how frightened I was, how I wondered if I had the outline well in mind, how I told myself that nervousness is a good thing, a sign of sensitivity, a real credential of concern for the job at hand! I often glanced down on the lectern, hoping to find a prompt sheet. I tried to visualize the notes that I had committed to memory, but over and over I kept telling myself that the great adventure was on.

The *will to try* had been triggered and the first forward step in a field I feared had been taken. Soon I no longer looked down for notes; I looked out into my audience for inspiration. Gradually, every public appearance became an adventure in which I pitted my ability, not against any protagonist, but against myself, my faith in myself, my faith in my subject, and my determination to communicate with those who had come to hear what I had to say. Soon the uplifted faces were no longer challenging and unfriendly; they were eager and interested, they were on my side, my adventure was theirs; and this is how I now feel about audiences whether it is a group of fifty in a college classroom or fifteen thousand in Madison Square Garden.

With few exceptions I agree with the admonition, "Do the thing you fear," and without any qualifications of any kind I would advise, "Make it an adventure." Ask yourself, "What is it I must overcome to be what I want to be?" Take an inventory and discover what it is that is holding you back from being your best and doing your best. Make it an adventure at this point and you will convert your weakness into your greatest strength. Strength comes with the doing.

The Spirit of Adventure
Can Be Your Spirit

I was in British Columbia when logger Bert Thomas announced that he would swim the dreaded Strait of Juan de Fuca. To some people this sounded like big talk. Thomas, twenty-eight, a former frogman with the U.S. Marines, had tried the eighteen-mile swim five times and had failed in every attempt. Other challengers, sixty-two in all, had also failed, and many had been dragged unconscious from the cold, kelp-tangled waters. But Bert Thomas insisted on trying again, and just before dawn walked into the cold, beating waves at Port Angeles, Washington. His destination was Victoria, British Columbia, and between him and that distant harbor were eddies and ebb currents and an undertow. Ringing in Bert's ears were the spurring words of his nine-year-old daughter who called to him, "Go, daddy, go!"

Newsmen and photographers no less than his trainer and admirers followed big Bert in boats through the slashing waves, watching his strong arms beat a rhythm through the swelling tide, counting his strokes, marking his time. Finally, at the end of the grueling uncharted eighteen-mile stretch, when the spectators themselves were fairly overcome by the torturous task, Bert Thomas walked out of the water under his own power through the waiting cheering crowds. He had been swimming steadily for eleven hours and ten minutes, but he was now the first man ever to have conquered the defiant Strait. Asked how he had done it, he replied, "I had my eye on Jerusalem. This shore was for me the Holy City. My daughter's words were my command."

Who could measure his feeling of achievement? Only he who has conquered the thing he fears or who has reached the goal he has set for himself can fully understand.

Take the case of a friend of mine who lost both legs in the war and who vowed that he would walk again and live a full life again and never apologize for being handicapped. With artificial limbs, he not only learned to walk, but to skate and dance and ski. On one occasion he entered a ski tournament and made a jump so spectacular that he almost won the event. He did win as far as his adventure with himself was concerned.

For sometimes you win even if you do not reach the goal. The members of the British mountaineering expedition, for example, who scaled the impossible slopes of Mt. Kangchenjunga in the Himalayas, third highest mountain in the world, won even though they stopped five feet short of the summit.

"Why did you stop?" people asked. "Why didn't you conquer those remaining five feet on the mountain that towers 28,146 feet into the misty sky?" The leader of the group explained why. "We respected the wishes and the feelings of the Sikkemese who regard the mountain as sacred and who asked us not to desecrate the summit of the gods."

Such is the spirit of adventure. The Scottish mountaineer, W. H. Murray, who led a reconnaissance party on Mt. Everest shortly before it was conquered, said, "Men will live in vain, however secure and comfortable their way of life, if they allow the spirit of adventure to die in their souls. When adventure dies, there can be no more progress in penetrating the strongholds of either Nature or of the Spirit."

There are levels of achievement. It is as great a thrill and no less an honor for a man to adjust to his job after he has considered his adjustment impossible as it is for a mountaineer to reach the glory of an unconquered peak.

Whatever you do, always adventure in your highest good.

4

Life is a series

of experiences

Life is a series of experiences, an adventurous game, and there are, of course, rules to be observed. One of these rules is that every individual has the privilege of certain rights. In our determination to exercise our own will, we often forget that the other person has his will and rights, too, as well as his ideas, which may clash with our own. To be aware of this can be a source of great strength to *you*. It will enable you to stand where the other person stands and can put you in a much stronger position to get along with him, to understand him, and to negotiate with him.

In any game, unfamiliarity with your opponent's techniques can spell your own defeat. You need to know not only your capabilities, but his. That is why scouts are invaluable in observing the plays of contending teams. They familiarize themselves thoroughly with the habits of the players, with their points of strength and weakness, and even with the most minor details that relate to the temperament and mood of the participants. In this way surprise plays are no longer surprises.

All of this is equally true in your relationship with the people with whom you live and work. Top-flight salesmen know their clients so well that they have established a rapport before they ever enter into business relations with them. A sales counsellor has made a fortune teaching others the grand art of this adventurous game. His theory is that every person has at least one basic all-absorbing interest in life. It may be a hobby or an intellectual pursuit, a frustrated longing, or any of a number of things. This one compelling interest the super-salesman refers to as his client's "hot button." His theory is that if you find out all you can about this "hot button" you will have established a strategic line of communication with your client.

Business managers, too, have learned to apply this approach. One industrial manager told me that a worker had been dismissed from two departments in the plant because of insubordination. The worker was labeled as a trouble-maker among the men and was finally asked to leave. Before he packed up, however, the manager in a heart-to-heart talk with the dismissed employee discovered that the only thing this man was really interested in was thinking up new ideas. He was a gadget-maker at heart and most of the days was thinking only about getting home to his hobby room where he could work out the ideas that came to him. The manager suggested that the man be given a place in the research department of the industry, although he had had no academic training for such a position. Nonetheless, the assignment was made and within three months this seemingly worthless worker had invented two appliances which eventually saved the industry over a quarter of a million dollars. What was equally important was that the man found himself and the industry found a man.

This synchronizing of one's aptitudes with a career is also a major factor in the lives of college students. In their early campus years many students are frustrated because of their vocational indirection. Despite all the aptitude tests and professional analyses to which they are subjected, no one has ever sat down with them and asked, "What would you like to do with your life above and beyond anything else in the world? If someone said to you, 'I will help you to do or to become whatever you wish,' what would you say?"

When a student synchronizes his deepest talent with his highest aspirations, I have often said, "All right, you can do it.

You have everything it takes: youth, opportunity, talent. All you need now is to be willing to pay the price for the training and enter into the adventure necessary to achieve the end." You cannot put a limit on talent, especially since it is generally agreed that 80% of genius is merely hard work! Of course, there are special capabilities and innate talents, but we rarely realize how much work, how many hours, and what great sacrifices have gone into the making of people whom we often envy or of whom we say, "Isn't he lucky?"

The Art of Not Looking Back

The zest for playing the game of life is often thwarted as we grow older, especially if there is a tendency to look back with remorse on "lost years." Many a person longs for a chance to relive the past, and a complaint I frequently hear is, "If I could only go back to school again and have the chance I once had but didn't appreciate!"

In the long run there are no lost years. Life is always a series of inter-related links in a chain of experiences and even though you may feel that certain periods were wasted and meaningless, they had karmic meaning, which is to say they helped make you what you are. Remember, too, that you may have exerted an influence upon other lives during those "lost years," an influence which had greater significance than you will ever know.

Today Is the Day

At any rate, there is no going back. Do not build remorse into the structure of your life by harping on what might have been. Do not go through life weighted down with something that cannot be undone. View existence not as part of a remorseful past or even as part of a more hopeful future, but as an eternal *now* challenging us to live this moment and every moment fully and richly and with a sense of great appreciation.

In a book which belonged to my father, he had written the date, 12/12/12, and under this designation he put this reminder: *This date will not happen again for a hundred years.* So it is with the present moment. It will not happen again, so make the most of it whatever the moment may be. Never regret, never feel frustrated for something that cannot be undone. Never look back on something that cannot be changed. There are things in life upon which the book must be closed. There are events out of which the last sentiment and meaning have been wrung. It is time now to look to the present and to stand anew, adventurously facing another day.

Take a Church on a Hill

A Catholic priest had an aversion to churches built on a hill. His parish was a friendly midwestern town on level land and he was happy about this. Hill churches, he contended were impractical, especially in winter when old people at the risk of life and limb had to drive or climb the icy slopes. Furthermore, he felt that it was patronizing for a house of God to be set apart and above the people whom it served. Having made quite an issue of this point and having expressed himself publicly on the matter, he was ordered by his bishop to a new parish some forty miles to the north. Sure enough, there stood a quaint white church, badly in need of repair, high on the highest hill.

The priest said to me, "When I saw it I stood at the bottom of the hill with my hands on my hips, just looking." But what could he do? He did what any obedient priest with an adventurous spirit would have done. He said, "I'm going to make this the loveliest church in town so that people looking at it will lift their eyes above it as I did, lift their eyes to the meaning beyond. I'm going to make it a place of service, and, what's more, I'll call it "The Church of the Open Way." With this he secured the cooperation of a group of his parishioners who vowed that, no matter what the weather, the path to the church would always be kept as easily accessible as possible. In summer it was flanked with rows of flowers and in winter it was shoveled clean and salted and cindered so that those who came caught the spirit of the adventure as they made their way upward to the house of God.

Or Take the Laborer at His Work

Every vocation affords an unlimited challenge for the truly dedicated worker if he remembers that life is a game and should be lived adventurously.

I spoke at a meeting in Detroit which was attended by men and women who manned the assembly lines in the motor industry. I had gone through these plants and had seen these people at work. I had stood in the midst of the incessant thunder of the machinery and had watched the hypnotic movement of the conveyors and the monotonous rhythm of the seemingly endless operations. Now, to my surprise, many of these laborers told me they saw in their work not monotony but opportunity. They were conscious of the noise, to be sure, but they had thoughts which transcended this bedlam. They were caught in the motion and the sounds, but some of them heard in them a symphony of our age in which they were an important and an integral part. They knew their work so well they felt like experts. They were paced to their hours of labor and when they were through they left their worries behind. They had interests far beyond those of the casual observer, and there was no limitation on their capacity for life.

There are managers and executives who at times secretly envy the laborer who does his job and then is free. There are many workmen who do not envy the industrialist one bit.

Life is what we make it right where we are and with what we have.

One of the happiest men I know is a trapper in the mountains of British Columbia. He envies no one, he covets nothing; his only aspiration is to be the best trapper in his section of the country. By best he does not mean the richest or even the best known. He means his orientation in his job. This reaches undreamed of proportions. His study of animals has made him so knowledgeable in this field that he has actually discovered another world. It has led him to an investigation of the environment in which the animals live and has taught him the names and uses of the native herbs and plants in the region. Out of it all has come an uncanny wisdom about nature and the out-of-doors, so much so that he is continually sought as a guide for men who wish to explore this mountainous country. Prospectors, hunters, climbers have beaten a path to the remote cottage where he lives, and people the length and breadth of the Kootenay country associate the name of George Oliver with the adventurous life.

Give Yourself a Thinking Period

Most of us realize only half of our possibilities and explore less than half of our potentials. We would do better if we spent more time in constructive reflection.

Many firms have "idea men" who are supposed to take up this slack in the creativity of companies and who suggest ways and means for greater achievement and expansion. Anyone connected with industry can come up with ideas if he will put his mind to it.

An executive of a large firm gives credit for his success to his "thinking period" every morning from eleven to twelve. During this hour he secludes himself in his office with instructions that he is not to be disturbed. In this uninterrupted period, he does nothing but *think*. Sometimes there is a period of meditation involved in this since he happens to be a very religious man. But the objective is to think creatively about his business and to explore experimentally the inrush of new ideas.

Think! Think of the trouble and difficulties you have become involved in because you didn't think! Perhaps the reason you didn't think is because you had no "thinking period." Before dropping off to sleep at night, ask yourself, "How much thinking did I do today?" You will be amazed to realize that ninety percent of your time was spent in mechanical acts, acts prompted by custom, by habit, by tradition. Talk about automation in industry! Nowhere has automation been carried further than in the individual life of every one of us. We have a built-in mechanism which grows more rigid as the years go by and only a "thinking period" can keep it flexible.

The wise old preacher said, "As a man *thinketh* in his heart so is he." We construe this as meaning that "you are what you think you are" and this is true enough, but Solomon may also have meant that thinking helps us to take an inventory of *why* we are what we are. Modern writers may have carried the idea too far, but the approach is fundamentally correct. "*Think* and grow rich," "*Think* thin and you will be thinner," "*Think* health and you will be healthier," "*Think* beauty and you will be more beautiful." *Think, think, think!*

Once there was a woman who had been annoyed for years in her housekeeping because of limited sundry needs. When she wanted a paper clip, she was usually out. When she needed a facial tissue in the kitchen, it was usually upstairs. When she wanted a pencil at the telephone, it was not there. When she looked for change for the paper boy, it was hard to find. One day she got to thinking. She made a list of all of these little annoyances, tucked $20 into her purse, went to town, and bought everything she needed, even to a little coin-changer which she kept in a handy drawer so that when the paperboy or the egg man came she had the right change ready at hand. It is amazing how many little irritations we live with from day to day simply because we do not stop to think how easily we can get rid of them.

Then There Is the Matter
of Self Dependence

While the trend these days is to share our troubles and to bare our concerns and thus get them off our minds, there is a good chance that we have gone too far in the use of this vicarious therapy. It is possible that in our reliance upon others, we have overlooked the reliability within ourselves. Certainly there is a feeling among many of us that we can buy our way out of trouble and be psychoanalyzed out of our concerns.

History will probably describe us as the willing victims of a welfare age. Homes pamper the children, schools pamper the students, the state pampers its citizens, and the nation pampers its people. For all this, we have sacrificed a certain ruggedness which has always been characteristic of the American way. And we have also thereby lost the spirit of adventure.

The greatest people are those who are free and we sacrifice a portion of our freedom each time we depend upon another for the things which we ourselves could do. Marxism's basic creed is, "From each according to his ability, to each according to his need." American democracy has a different principle: "Let each develop according to his ability and let all have equal opportunity to alleviate their need."

The Someday Psychosis

An uncle of mine got to be a very rich man, but as long as he lived he never did the things he secretly longed to do. I can see him now seated at his roll-top desk in the Sauk City State Bank above which hung a yellowing map of the European continent. There were, I remember, finger marks on Switzerland where he had often pointed out his ancestral home with the brave remark, "Someday I'm going over there." But he never went. I can see him now on a Wisconsin winter's day bundled to the teeth in his wraps as he came into the bank to begin another day. There he stood in a warm corner of the drafty room toying with the gold watch fob on the chain spun across his vest. I can still hear him say, "Someday Pauline and I are going to take a real vacation somewhere where it's warm." But they never did.

It may be my revolt against this Someday Theory that has prompted me to do the things I really want to do, to take the trips I really want to take, and to see the things I really want to see. The small town where I grew up was filled with "someday" people and I continually find others in my travel and research who content themselves, often bitterly, with a "someday" hope.

From the man who someday hopes to improve his place in life to the woman who someday hopes to slenderize, there is a whole wide world of individuals who have a future in escrow which they will never use.

It applies as well to little things. The drab room over which you sigh, "Someday I'll have to do some decorating." The garage door against which you've scraped many a fender. "Someday I'll have to widen that!" The flower garden where the daffodils have been getting scrawnier year by year, the filing cabinet which has long since become a morgue of forgotten things—all waiting the eternal *someday*.

While these procrastinators may be dreaming of high adventure on some windswept hill, there is a challenge waiting for them in their own backyard and in their own clothes closets, to say nothing of the basement or the attic. The task at hand no less than the will to travel becomes more difficult in direct proportion to the time of deferment. If you put off the slenderizing process long enough, you will learn to live philosophically with your bulges. Of course, this may be an adventure in itself and deep down in your subconscious it may be exactly what you wish to do! You be the judge.

Thinking of how some people have met and conquered their "someday" challenges, I remember particularly a young mother who had the misfortune of losing three children at birth and who was warned by her doctor that it would be extremely dangerous for her ever to attempt to have another child. She replied, "But someday I will have one," and she set about immediately negotiating for an adoption. She made this her adventure despite the disheartening delays involved in such a procedure. Rewarded with a beautiful baby girl, she proved to be such an extraordinary mother that she had no difficulty in subsequently adopting two more children to complete her family.

Life, as we said, is a series of experiences. It is a game and the rules of the game say that you are rewarded according to the way you play it.

5

Your adventure and you

While travel usually involves adventure, adventure by no means needs to involve travel. A classical example is found in the life of Christ. He spent his thirty-three years within a radius of fifty miles from his home. He amassed no fortune. He never aspired to worldly fame.

Yet, though He traveled little, there was no place on earth to which His mind did not reach. Though He had no material wealth, He had spiritual possessions incapable of being appraised. Though He asked for no worldly acclaim, His spirit inspired all who seriously reviewed His life. In Him is a symbol of the adventurous spirit characteristic of all prophets who left their impression on mankind. Studying their lives we find that their qualities, their faith, their philosophies help us in an understanding of ourselves. They always recognized great resources within themselves. They considered no problem insurmountable and they utilized every experience to gain a better understanding of their mission in life.

We would do well to read the biographies of the so-called great. Of course, this in itself constitutes an adventure and a discipline, for it means that we must set aside a portion of every day for this kind of self-development. But it can be done.

A friend of mine figured out that he wasted at least three

hours each day in the sheer mechanics of the day's activities. For example, waiting for the bus, waiting to be served in a restaurant, whiling away time on nonessentials, watching meaningless TV programs, listening to the radio just to be killing time, even going to bed before he was actually tired. So he decided to carry with him pocket editions of inspirational writings. Even though he read only a paragraph or two, he soon discovered that he was gaining an education and tapping a source of knowledge that were influencing and enriching his life. It is amazing how much time we fritter away and how many meaningless things we do just to be passing time. Today we have such easy access to the literary wealth of the world that there is no excuse for us not to share in it.

Familiarize yourself with the lives of the founders of the world's great faiths, commit yourself to studying one a week, and at the end of two short months, you will have a comprehension of what most of the three billion people in the world believe and live by! You will understand better why they act as they do, and what their hopes for this life and the life to come involve. What is more, such a study will prove an exciting adventure.

Or take the matter of languages. I know people who have learned a foreign language in their spare time—in time that was ordinarily dissipated. If you were to learn only three foreign words a day, in a year you would have a vocabulary that would carry you through a country where this language is spoken. It is no secret that many people who have good vocabularies have developed them by adding only one new word a day. In the morning before they begin their work, they look up a word in the dictionary and during the day they use it in conversation or in writing. In this way they make it a part of their knowledgeable life.

The same technique holds true of those "well-read" individuals who every morning take time to open an encyclopedia and familiarize themselves with a certain area of knowledge and then at night read it again to fix it in their consciousness as part of a worthy, self-educational process. Actually the most successful people are the self-made people, for while a formal education may be imperative, the self-training, discipline, and wisdom which are self-engendered are, in the long run, most vital.

It was noted recently that Thomas Edison would have a difficult time passing the entrance exams in an accredited modern school of science were he living today. This may be true. Undoubtedly there are vast areas of theoretical knowledge, historical data, and modern terminology with which he would have to struggle, but Edison had the will to learn and to work and to develop his creative powers and all of this we, too, can do if we have the determination. The world goes forward on the shoulders of people of this kind, and they can be found in every field of endeavor. Most of all, there is the satisfaction of having unlocked within yourself the slumbering genius of your own great capability.

"Know Thyself"

I have often theorized that every person is a genius in something. The trick is to discover what that something is and where that genius lies. How do you know but that you might be the greatest violinist in the world if you have never had a violin under your chin? How do you know but that somewhere in your nature may be concealed a profound talent for, let us say, horticulture or mathematics or astronomy? You may be the greatest horse-shoe-pitcher in the world, but how do you know if you have never tried? Of course, the question is, "If I am talented in some strange and remote field, why have I never been led to discover that talent?" There is at least one answer to this question. Life, for reasons untold—unless it is to give zest and interest to life—is an unending quest. Life is in every respect a process of search and discovery.

Since time began man has found this to be true. Life continually confounds us with mystery. We have never fully solved the riddle. We build ever greater telescopes in the hope of measuring the universe only to discover that the greater the telescope the greater the universe. Man splits the atom and discovers the microcosm of the universe sealed within the unseen. It is estimated that physical man consists of a combination of over five billion cells and that a blood stream three miles long circulates in his body. He knows that atoms form molecules, molecules form cells, cells form tissues, and tissues form man, and when he has said all of this, he must still ask, "What is the basis of life?" It is a quest, and therein lies the thrill and the glory of living.

"Know thyself" is the keyword in all philosophies and the great command of all the greatest minds. Explore your life, the life that is yours alone. Face it honestly, squarely, sincerely, and decide for yourself whether there is not a great mine of talent and potential which has never been quarried. We use only a small portion of our mental faculties, we are told, but we use even less of our *will* to be the great person we can be if we are unwilling to take the first adventurous step.

What Is Greatness?

A further word must be said about this greatness, for it is so easy to misunderstand its meaning. There are great people and then there are simply notorious people. There are people who leave an impression on others, and there are those who are merely good press copy. No doubt the greatest people are those who leave their world a little better than they found it and certainly many of these individuals never got their names in the headlines.

You can test this in your own acquaintance. In the community or neighborhood where you live is there someone whose quiet influence is shaping the structure of the community, someone whom you instinctively turn to when you need inspiration, help, or advice? One of the most influential people of this kind whom I know is a woman who has lived all of her ninety years unobtrusively in a small mid-western town. Because of the need for caring for her parents, she never married. Because of circumstances, she earned no college degree. Because of a

quiet, retiring nature, she remained unnoticed beyond Hometown. Yet there is nothing in that community today which does
not show the stabilizing influence of "Aunt Elizabeth." The
schools, the churches, the library, the homes have all caught
something of her selfless nature. Her contributions financially,
culturally, and spiritually were made in such an unobtrusive
way that the spirit of the giving was even greater than the
gift itself. Few young people return to the village without
dropping around for a visit with her. Her homespun philosophy
has been carried into far distant lands. Her genius is that she
simply plays her part as a good citizen; that she has found
a faith in which she believes, a philosophy in which she trusts,
and a quietude which she feels God wants her to express.

The secret of "Aunt Elizabeth's" life is "interest without
intrusion." She is constantly alert and alive to all of the issues
in the town. Her balanced judgment, unswayed by any thought
of personal gain, makes people seek her out. Her inner strength
rubs off—makes the weak feel stronger, and calms the agitated.

These, of course, are qualities we all possess to some degree
and it is up to us to decide how far we wish to develop them.
We all have substantially the same potentials. Granted that
some people are smarter than others, we all have an intelligence
quotient which can be improved. Granted that some people
are more handsome than others, everyone has intrinsic beauty
which can be enhanced. Although everyone has a certain degree
of extrasensory perception, those who truly wish to do so may
sharpen theirs if they are ready to give to the development
the time required. In every case work and effort are involved,
and even faith works best where you work at your faith.

Speaking of Talents

Recently I heard of a man who had exceptional ability as a
woodcarver. A visit to his home convinced me that he was on
his way to becoming a master craftsman. "I was forced into
this almost to save myself," he said and then told me his story.
He was a day laborer in a mine, assigned to the job of "dial

watcher." For eight monotonous hours a day his assignment was to sit at a desk in front of a wall and watch a huge dial whose indicators showed where and at what levels the cages carrying the workmen were located at any given moment. When the foreman on one of the levels changed the position of a cage, an alarm sounded on the dial and simultaneously a light flashed, warning the dial watcher through sight and sound what was going on deep below the earth.

There he sat with nothing to do but to watch the various positions so that in the event of a disaster the workmen could be notified. He had been warned never to fall asleep. He had been cautioned not to read lest he become so engrossed that neither the alarm nor the light would arouse him. He was just supposed to sit, confronted by the agonizingly hypnotic eyes of the dial. How could he make a job like this adventurous? He did it by a process of analysis and discovered that in carving out wooden figures he could sublimate the monotony of his job in a creative pursuit. The drab dial room became his private studio, and he looked forward to his hours "on the job." Other men with less determination and less imagination had been known to lose their minds after prolonged work in this room. This man made of it a harmonious surrounding, and in the process he is becoming an expert craftsman, a wood-carver of unusual note.

Work Is What You Make It

Since my first love is writing, I was often frustrated when my academic job necessitated extended travel. "If only I could remain at my desk and write!" Then I learned that I could combine travel and writing, and today I always carry with me on the seat of the car a clipboard and sharpened pencils. Driving is unusually conducive to generating ideas and it seems to me that many of my best pages have been written on the side of the road or in an unlikely parking lot! Trains and planes can also become a writer's workshop if he is willing so to convert them by the magic of his mind.

Your Work and You

Success is first of all a matter of liking your job. If you do not enjoy what you are doing, you will never give the work your best effort. Just as in marriage it is necessary to love your mate, and in sports it is necessary to love the game, so in any successful vocation you must love your work. This becomes easier if you remember that every assignment has both a sur-face approach and an approach in depth. Communication media have over-used the term "news in depth" but most of us have underestimated the concept of "work in depth" which means that we should grasp the universal implications of the job at hand and add to it our affection for interpreting these im-plications.

I have had the good fortune of making my work my hobby because of my love for every phase of it. That is why I feel that everyone should find work which is so satisfying that the enjoyment of it itself becomes a reward quite apart from the monetary consideration. Many a baseball star has remarked with candid humor, "I enjoy playing so much it's a wonder they pay me for it!" Paradoxically those who like what they are doing are more successful and make more money than those who try to make money in jobs they do not like. It is some-thing like first "seeking the kingdom" and then having "all things added unto you."

When a man loses himself in his commitment, he will be doubly blessed because of his dedication. We all know indi-viduals who seem to have the Midas touch and whose success and prosperity seemed to come with amazing ease. Their effort-less approach to life is often a source of frustration and mystery to their observers. Can it be that there is some power which so befriends a man when he turns his material needs over to the working of a law that he is rewarded beyond all proportion to what the average person might expect? Is it possible that love for one's work, love for what one is doing, and love for the sense of achievement of purpose may actually be the basis for material well-being? And can it be that we have been putting the cart before the horse all too long by thinking first of "how much is in it for me?"

Our Freedom to Work

My freedom to write as I wish, to choose my vocation, and to make the most of my life are precious heritages of the American Way which I have learned to appreciate more because of travel in other countries.

Although people in other lands also carve out their destinies and are sometimes more free than we realize, no other nation gives its people the right to adventure as does the U.S.A. Every single individual in this land of ours can find a place in which to invest his talents and profit from them if he is willing to work, to be alert to opportunities, and to spend time in creative thinking.

This freedom of opportunity is, in a very real way, the greatest freedom we have. Granted that there are good breaks and bad ones that come to all of us, there is also always a line of cause and effect which, if honestly traced, will provide the clue to what we customarily call Fate or Chance.

Behind every great enterprise is the vision of an individual who, with the age-old ingredients of courage and faith, blueprinted the project.

There were moments in the lives of the developers and founders of our industries when their greatest conferences were held not around a table with a board of directors but rather with themselves—alone. They asked themselves some penetrating questions. "How sincere am I in this project? What do I really hope to achieve? How do my principles of operation stack up against the ideals I hold to be true and inviolable? Where am I heading? How sincerely am I using my talents?"

These and many other criteria are continually on the agenda of every consecrated life. This does not apply to big businessmen or industrialists alone. Every honest workman, laborer, farmer, or professional man is confronted by the touchstone of such thoughts when he embarks on the adventurous life.

This is how the well-known Four-Way Test was born. It was born when Rotarian Herb J. Taylor squarely faced himself and his vocation and asked:

1. Is it the Truth?
2. Is it Fair to all concerned?
3. Will it build Good Will and Better Friendships?
4. Will it be Beneficial to all concerned?

From that moment on a philosophy evolved which formed the basis for his operations.

Freedom to Believe

We desperately need a philosophy tailored to fit our highest selves and patterned after the highest ideals we are capable of achieving. There is no reason to believe that this philosophy must perfectly coincide with the beliefs of others. Who is to say that one man's sense of right is higher than another's? In the great game of life, we must play our role with what we have, with where we are, and with the principles in which we truly believe. With these basic rules, let us keep our minds ever open to improvement, change, and the inter-penetration of new truths.

All of this comes close to man's spiritual experience which we will discuss later on, but it should be said at this point that the spiritual quest is first of all a personal encounter. The church can help immeasurably and the fellowship of faith is not to be denied. Spirituality is, as Harry Emerson Fosdick once said, "an individual psychological experience."

I am continually meeting individuals whose lives were changed when this personalization of the quest became real for them, when they no longer worried about the direction of other people's lives but realized their job was giving their own lives direction. Little people spend most of their time evaluating other people rather than generating new ideas. The biggest people spend most of their time evaluating and investing their potentialities.

This does not mean a neurotic evaluation or analysis; neither does it mean a pathological pampering of ourselves. It means, rather, investing one's life in areas where effort and talent will count most. Truly successful people get themselves off their own hands by selfless dedication to some great purpose. It is as if the Super Self or the mystical alter ego (the Second Self) stepped forward to direct the smaller self in these activities. Self with a capital "S" is the master and manager of the conscious self which waits only a command to do the Super Self's bidding. Such an implication is found in the maxim about losing one's life in order to find it.

The Self and the Self

How often have you said to yourself, "You should do this," or "You should not have done this," or "You should think this over." You may even have called yourself by name and said, "Now, listen, is this really what you want to do?" The greater ego was commanding the lesser, the Self was addressing the self.

Have you ever tried "setting your mind" to do your bidding? Some people, adept at this, can, for example, command their mind to wake them at a certain time. They develop a sort of mental alarm clock which works for them infallibly. Before going to sleep, they say, "I will awake at exactly six o'clock," and at six o'clock the trusty mental timepiece rouses them. Others carry it further. They say, "Today at noon some good fortune will happen to me." Or early in the morning they set their minds on specific things they wish to have happen and they have claimed wonderful results through such pre-determining. Since hypnosis has proved the many marvels of the mind and has authoritatively controlled some of the most phenomenal post-hypnotic suggestions, is there not a possibility that *self*-hypnosis or positive suggestibility may also work some extraordinary miracles in life?

All is part of the adventure. You can make money at it, too, for if you think prosperity thoughts, you will automatically get your mind off thoughts of poverty and set up thoughts of abundance which not only change your thinking but direct your actions into more prosperous channels. This is one of the basic formulas involved in tithing experiments. If you set aside a certain portion of your money for benevolent purposes, chances are that your entire financial outlook will take on a new orderliness.

This is not to say that a plus factor of mysticism is missing in the tithing experiment, but even apart from this there is the tested psychological fact that our determination to be good stewards rewards us with a desire for more systematic accounting in our economy. Make it an adventure in your financial life. Try to strike a balance between frugality and extravagance. The man who truly adventures is not limited by being too overly cautious nor does he fall prey to being overly reckless in the conduct of his affairs.

An ultra-conservative friend of mine who has never been noted for his charity once said to me, "Look, what I found on my way to work this morning," and he pulled a crumpled $5 bill from his pocket. I said to him, "Give it away. The Lord probably wants you to give it to some worthy cause." "Heck, no!" was the reply. "If the Lord didn't want me to keep it, why did He let me find it in the first place?"

Well, it was a point of view and we often joked about it, but I noticed that he did begin to engage in several charitable acts, as if caught in an adventure with which he had never experimented in the past. Just for the fun of it, everyone should have at least four experiences somewhere along the way of life:

1. Fall in love.
2. Have a wisdom tooth extracted.
3. Invest in some speculative stock.
4. Do a great and good deed anonymously.

You Never Can Tell
Where Adventure Will Lead!

During the days of the depression in the thirties many sharp real estate men persuaded midwestern farmers to invest in Florida land. The salesmen said (although they didn't really believe it) that a big boom was coming and they appealed to the spirit of adventure in their prospective buyers. Many a farmer bought land in those days without ever having seen it. Most of it was isolated, wild terrain, and some of it was even under water. But they made it an adventure, a sort of blind adventure, and they bought it, and the land sharks went gleefully on their way. Nonetheless, most of the purchasers hung on to the questionable property, ashamed to admit that they had been so taken in. Some ten years later a boom did come, Florida cities expanded, earth-moving and drainage machinery reclaimed rough and submerged acres, and the farmers suddenly became land barons, even boasting now that they had it figured out all along! Life, like land, is a game and its fortune moves in cycles.

You never can tell where your adventure will lead!

6

Take a storybook look

at yourself

An effective way to make your life an adventure is to look at your experiences in terms of a book, a novel, or a story. Not that you are necessarily going to write the book, but when you look at life as an author looks at his material, every event and every circumstance takes on a new dimension.

One day a South Dakota school teacher complained that her job was getting her down. She had recently been caught in a blizzard in her isolated schoolhouse and was snowed in for seven days. So were her thirteen pupils.

I said, "What a story!"

"What do you mean 'what a story?' " she retorted. "I almost went out of my mind!"

"Think of the dramatic material," I insisted. "Snowed in with thirteen pupils in a 12′ × 20′ room for a solid week! Think of the people who envy you for such an adventure. Think of the human interest, the things the kids did and said, the resourcefulness you had to demonstrate, the funny as well as the tragic things that must have happened!"

"Well," she confessed, "I wouldn't give up the experience for anything, but I don't want to go through it again."

That is exactly the point. The highlights of life have a price tag. If they did not, we would soon forget them. We should look at our extraordinary situations as a writer looks at life, then the events take on new meaning and interest, then we get a new look at what might be merely irritating occasions. Then bad breaks become plot situations. Good breaks are encounters with a happy fate. Day-by-day affairs turn into a drama played for the joy of the playing. Life takes on a new thrill. When you come right down to it, there is a book that only you can write: the story of your life. And even if you never put it down on paper, write it on your heart.

A coal miner in Harlan, Kentucky, told me some of his impressions while working on the job. Although he never wrote them down, whenever he went underground he pretended that he was a playwright who, in his mind's eye, saw a drama unfold and felt its wonders.

"I get a strange sort of feeling working down there," he said. "Especially at night. The dark is always the same, but the earth stirs different at night. You hear it stirring. The dust drops around you like stars out of the black. You hear groans as if the earth was tired and wanted to stretch. I've thought many-a-time that if I'd listen real quiet I might of heard the voice of God."

Take a new look at *your* life and get a new line on *your* job. Things that now seem monotonous and dull take on a different slant if you think of them in terms of a book, the book that only you can write. This is the secret behind successful novels; they grow out of experiences that were looked at through storybook eyes and then transmitted into interesting objective accounts. Writers are people who interpret their personal adventures and impressions on a universal scale. They look at them on a huge canvas, and that is what you should do with your life and your job. But, again, you do not have to write the book; all you need to do is to look at your place in the scheme of things as one of the greatest stories ever told.

Every Life Is a Story

My encouragement to try my hand at writing came from author Lloyd Douglas. We were having dinner at the Amana

Colonies in Iowa, and I was telling him about the history of
the Amanas and other little-known collectivistic experiments.

"Why don't you write about your experiences among these
groups?" Mr. Douglas asked. "You have some rich material."

That is what I needed, someone to light the fuse, someone
to tell me that my life and my work reached a depth deeper
than I realized, someone to show me the acres of diamonds
under my feet, to take me by the hand, as it were, and point out
the beauty of surroundings which had become commonplace
because of my familiarity with them.

Douglas spoke from experience. He had been just another
clergyman in Canada, and his work could have remained
merely routine. He could easily have closed his eyes to the
fact that every life is a story and that his life, because it was
his, could be made the most exciting of all. His first great
literary success, *Magnificent Obsession,* was a story that only
he could tell, packed with emotions that he had felt, filled
with a longing that was part of his life. When he sent the
manuscript to the publishers, he included a comment, "I don't
know whether this is any good or not, but it is something I
simply had to write."

Rarely do I sit down with a young writer without telling
him what Lloyd Douglas said to me, "You have some rich
material." Everyone has rich material if he thinks in terms of
his own life, because every life is unique, every life is a particular expression for a specific period in space and time. Your
life is like that. Your life is a story and you in a very real way
are the writer of its pages. Make it an adventure.

A New Look at America

No country on earth gives its people the opportunity that
we find in the U.S.A. As you take a new look at yourself, see
yourself against the background of our fifty freedom-born
states.

Something of a climax in this new appraisal was reached
on February 20, 1962, when Colonel John H. Glenn, Jr. made

his three orbital flights around the earth. We had criticized the press for its earlier insistence that every possible phase of the flight should be covered. We had sold ourselves short in the light of achievements in outer space by the U.S.S.R. Then our turn came and from early morning until late at night we saw the spirit of America unfold. We discovered how American teams work together, how American people respond together, how American youth react together, and how American hearts give thanks together under the cherished freedom of the American Way.

Ours is the spirit of adventure. It has always been so, though we may at times have abused and misused it. It has always been the hallmark of our culture. It has always been our heritage, though we may have often taken it lightly. It has always been our hope, though we may frequently have despaired that we were letting it slip away. And the spirit of adventure which is America is your spirit.

And a New Look at Leisure

No country in the world gives its people as high a living standard as does America, nor do any people have the leisure which we have no matter what our job or what our status in life may be.

This fact makes it imperative that we know how to use our leisure wisely. An ever shorter work week, more money, and more time for ourselves are blessings only if we have the wisdom to invest them in constructive and adventurous pursuits.

Some of the most restless and discontented people I know are those who have time on their hands and no idea what to do with it. With days to squander, they surfeit themselves with all sorts of escape contrivances. One of these malcontents once told me, "I thought I would be the happiest person in the world if I could spend my life playing bridge, but if you know that you can play all the bridge you want the game loses its charm."

People who are on a continuous vacation lose the richest experience of a vacation period which is, of course, an interlude in one's routine, workaday life. If you have two or three weeks a year for your holiday period you will plan for it with more enthusiasm than if you have months to squander.

It is a great day when we learn never to envy anyone and when we recognize the fact that our life can be richly lived on its own particular level. Not that we should lose our ambition or our aspiration to have the "better things of life" or leisure and opportunities, but we delude ourselves when we say, "If I were only in his place!" or "If I only had her way of life!" or "If only I had three months off instead of three weeks!"

Every life has the same challenges, problems, and situations and the encounter with these circumstances is always relative. We find proof of this in our own lives. When we were children, we said, "If I could only be in my teens!" When that time came, we longed to be adults. Being adults, we looked forward to independence and security, and as we grew older and had the things we wished for and dreamed of in youth, we were by no means as content as we assured ourselves we would be if ever we reached this point.

My mother, like so many other people, never found her truest happiness because her unfinished dreams of the future blinded her to the fulfilled dreams of the present. She was quite aware of this and often tried to make this awareness her adventure. Frequently she took refuge in Douglas Malloch's poem, "When Life Is Best," in which he soliloquizes about the glory of life in all its ages and phases and concludes by saying:

> Every stone
> Along life's way has a joy its own;
> If gold your hair or white your brow,
> Your happiest years are always *now*.

For many years I was heir to my mother's restless discontent. My ambition to write, after my meeting with Mr. Douglas, was so intense that I vowed if I could ever see just one of my very own books on the shelf, that was all I would ask of life.

I remember the thrill when the first copy came from the publisher. I shall never forget the slick and shiny jacket and the good feeling I had of having compressed a bit of the stuff of life into those crisp and friendly pages. Then almost immediately I thought how lonely that one book looked and how it needed a companion. Today there is a shelf full. While I must confess that a new book, like a new child, never ceases to provide a thrill, I do sometimes wonder if even birth, be it books or babies, may not be overdone. Certainly the events become commonplace unless one looks upon each expression, upon each new creation, and upon each new life as an adventure rich and vital within itself.

Keep a Fresh Approach

"When your job fails to challenge you," an employer told his men, "get into something else."

This may be sound advice as far as it goes and worthy of considerable thought. Surely, many a person has grown stale and listless in a job he once found challenging. But circumstances will not always permit a change. Everyone has his moments of occasional discontent whether it is a housewife over her kitchen sink or an industrialist at his polished desk. But there cannot always be escape or running away. The greatest adventure may be to re-explore one's job and to creatively discover how it can be taken out of the commonplace and looked upon as a new and fresh approach.

I was in a suite of offices recently where a complete re-decorating job was in progress. The director of the organization said he had given his staff permission to re-design their offices according to their own tastes. He had noticed that they had become lackadaisical and restless in their surroundings, and it dawned upon him that he had never let them create an environment according to their own ideas. He said, "They spend as much time in these offices as they do in their homes and I wouldn't presume to dictate what their homes should be like." His decision to let them plan their own surroundings was a sound, workable procedure, and it ushered in a new and lively spirit among his staff.

There is always a re-emphasis on individual freedom in all its many phases. Much of this may be a revolt against totalitarian threats to curb men's freedoms. There is a danger, however, that in our lust for total liberty we may be neglecting certain disciplines and responsibilities which are necessary for self development, and we may be overlooking certain insights which are needful for self determination.

Change your job by all means if you are fed up with it and if you can improve your lot in life, but do not do so without asking yourself whether the full potential of your present position has been honestly appraised and fully realized.

Where to Find
the Greatest Treasure

There is an interesting parallel in my study of religions. Often a person leaves his parental faith without ever having explored its teachings. Frequently he runs away from the very treasure he is seeking. Change is not always improvement. It is not newness alone which provides the answers. More often it is a second look at your old estate.

A legend retold in every generation and in every culture tells how the gods on Mt. Olympus once met to determine where they should hide man's divinity. "For," said the gods, "man's greatest adventure will be the search and discovery of this elusive factor." One god suggested that it be hidden in the sea, another in the clouds, and a third proposed that it be buried deep within the earth. It was then that the oldest and the wisest of the gods proclaimed, "Gentlemen, let us hide man's divinity in the heart of man himself, for that is the last place he will ever think of looking for it."

A Simple Secret of Success

As the discovery of one's divinity involves the personal venture, so does the discovery of the secret of success. Success is also an inside job. Everyone is telling us that to be successful one must think success, be in harmony with success, and anticipate success. This is true, but there are also ways and means of bringing about success. For one thing, to do a little more than the job expects of you may be one of the very greatest of secrets. Many people are content to do what the job requires of them and even a little less if possible. Consequently, a person who does a little *more* is automatically recognized and singled out as an extraordinary person.

Nowhere is this more noticeable than in the area of domestic services. The gardener who drops around on an off day to check the hedge he has trimmed, the waitress who gives you a little special attention, the newsboy who on a rainy day makes sure the paper is delivered clean and dry, the service station operators who vacuum your car, the baker who puts in an extra bun or gives you the proverbial baker's dozen; these people have become so rare that when we find them we happily tell others about our discovery and honor them with our patronage. That these extras pay off is obvious, and why they are not used more universally is a mystery.

The other day I made a purchase in a store and the bill was $8.11. It happened that I had $8.10. "I am sorry," said the cashier, "I need another penny." I had been searching my pockets in vain and said, "Sorry, but the smallest I have is a five." "Well," was the response, "I gues I'll just have to take it out of that." And she did. I have often thought how easily this cashier might have bought a good deal of good will by investing a penny of her own in the business!

Businesses, like individuals, are readily identified by a character trademark. It symbolizes what they have been, what they are, and what they plan to be in the future. It is their "image." And the image, though a much over-used word, is the precious, nonsaleable, nontransferable ingredient that can make or break an individual or a firm. The spirit of adventure, whether it is investing a penny or a life in the business, is the vital force in the corporate structure, and it shines through whatever that business does in its service field.

Keep the Spirit Strong

Life, then, is a matter of an approach, an attitude, a point of view.

In the beginning we talked about *wangas* and *paquets*. It was pointed out that we are controlled not by circumstances as much as by our mental attitude when circumstances arise. This mental attitude requires work, and frequently a change of mind, and often a determination to direct ourselves into the channel of our highest good. The determining factor is a matter of the will.

We can be content with our lot in life or we can rise above it; we can stay as we are or we can go on to greater things; we can be mastered by situations or we can master them.

A Negro religious leader, the much publicized Father Divine, suggested a technique to his followers which worked small miracles in people's lives. He persuaded his converts to itemize their problems and shortcomings, to actually write them down and take a good hard look at them. Sins committed, offenses done to others, petty thefts over which the grass had grown, all should be jotted down. This done, the individuals were inspired by Father Divine to make restitution and amends for these items one by one until the slate was clean. Those who took this seriously discovered that their lives were notably changed.

The very fact of listing one's problems, misdeeds and frustrations has a therapeutic effect. When we look at them squarely we bring them out of the realm of the abstract. We can deal with them now as one deals with a visible opponent. Some situations may prove to be more formidable than we realized, but others will only become non-essential illusions which our imagination had grossly enlarged. If you were to make a list of this kind right now, what problem would lead the parade of annoyances or difficulties haunting your life? How about asking yourself, "How can my own adventurous spirit cope with these situations? Have I ever met these situations honestly? Have I ever faced them squarely?"

Make it an adventure! This is the gist of the whole idea in coming to terms with yourself. No one will do it for you. No one will take the initiative for you. No one will step forward and say, "I want to carry the load for you." Even the tantalizing words which are at the heart of the Christian gospel, "Come unto Me" imply that there is a personal work to be done, restitutions to be made, forgiveness to be asked, and future struggles still to be encountered. Life continually involves these assignments and we should not ask to be spared from them if we would live fully and richly.

There is a great similarity between the exercise of the spirit and the exercise of the body, and he who continually refuses to flex his spiritual muscles will naturally become flabby of soul.

What we are aiming at is a method by which we can live our best and do our best and walk through the world courageously and unafraid. These goals cannot be reached if we approach our situations fearfully or avoid them cleverly or deny them unrealistically.

Look about you, see for yourself how the adventurous spirit changes people, how it spells the difference between a zest for life and a bored acceptance of life, how it spurs men on to great achievements while others stand still, how it lifts people out of the commonplace, makes every day a new beginning, transforms men's jobs, gives them something to live for, and makes the world the thrilling place it was meant to be!

Why are we here if not to make the most of life, to sense the hidden beauty, to explore the hidden depths, to unlock the hidden doors? Why are we here in a universe still waiting to be discovered and an inner life still waiting to be known and secrets upon secrets still waiting to be solved, if not to be challenged by all the potentials which are ours?

How quickly the years pass and with what remorse we look back upon the past! How often must we be told that the greatest time is this time, the most wonderful hour is this hour, the most vital moment is this moment! How often have we been caught up in a sudden ecstatical experience as if it were a glimpse of what life can really be, only to lapse again into the wanton notion that such a world may not be for us or that it must always be but temporary or fleeting? Perhaps such glimpses of a better-than-this-world cannot be the constant tone of life, but they are hints of worlds within worlds and life within life—which can be yours if you will but dare to make it an adventure!

PART TWO

The Social Adventure

7

Your new neighborhood: the world

During the orbital flight of astronaut John Glenn, I had to walk from my office to the post office to mail a letter. This required fifteen minutes. In that time the astronaut went from somewhere over Africa to somewhere over the Indian Ocean. While I walked back to the office he went one-third the distance around the earth.

As orbital flights continue, as men span the uncharted oceans of space, and as ever-faster jets give us earthlings our own magical wings, a new and intimate world takes on reality. We are all part of this amazing adventure. The new world a-coming is yours and mine and in a very real way it is being explored for you and me.

In a homespun way I was prepared for this world long ago when, as a boy, I heard my father say, "As the world becomes smaller, we must all become bigger."

He was a businessman and the remark was prompted when he brought home from his store a bolt of silk from Siam. In those days Siam was more remote than the moon is now, and I knew as little about it as I now know about Mars. Bangkok, the capital of Siam, was a legendary place along with such cities as Baghdad, Singapore, Constantinople, and Damascus.

I sometimes wonder whether Father himself knew what he was saying or whether he actually foresaw the unimaginable phenomenon of our shrinking world? Perhaps he did, for our hometown was changing in those days as America is changing now. New people were continually moving in. New industries were being established. The village we had always known as a somewhat exclusive community was being invaded. Its intimacy was ruffled by "outsiders" who had a wish and a will to be "insiders" along with the rest of us.

Religiously the town had been evenly divided between Roman Catholics and Protestants and the lines were clearly drawn. Everyone knew everyone else and knew, too, where their neighbors stood so far as religion, politics, and social status were concerned.

All this was now being altered. Our community was becoming more compact, and it demanded bigger people, people who could see beyond their own narrow ideologies. As a small town merchant my father may have been forced into this larger view. It was only good business to treat all new-comers as potential customers, but I suspect he saw something beyond the dollar sign. After all, he had reached out to touch Siam.

As he spread the cloth on the table and as we gazed wide-eyed at the intricate design, it was like looking at the multi-colored Biblical cards which in those days we carried home with us from Sunday School. The cards were not quite real either. Babylon, Nineveh, and Canaan were so far away in space and time that neither they nor their people ever came to life. Even my deeply religious mother could not make these cities or these people come alive. The world's population was conveniently put into rigid classes: foreigner and native, Oriental and Caucasian, Jew and Gentile, pagan and Christian, primitive and civilized, good and bad. It was a big world— a big, mysterious, and forbidding world.

But then there was Siam.

Siam is Thailand now, and when last I was there I brought home a rubbing from a temple, put it in my study, and sat for a long time thinking about our changing world. There are temple horns from Tibet in my study, pictures from India, artifacts from Cambodia, figurines from Hong Kong, shrine pieces from China and Japan, a mezuzah from Israel, a Moslem "rosary" from the Middle East, cruets from Rome, a Russian icon, a book from Pakistan, a cross from Jericho, masks from Yucatan, a drum from Haiti, a picture of Dr. Albert Schweitzer taken during my African visit . . . . all reminding me that the world, your world and mine, is now a neighborhood.

"As the world becomes smaller, we must all become bigger" may be just another way of saying that we must all learn to live together or no one will live. But it means something more. It suggests adventure and a new perspective in our relationship with our fellowmen.

See Your World
As an Exciting World

Take, for example, a college campus. Today there is hardly a school which does not have a large quota of international students. Young people from the major nations of the world are represented, and the opportunity for cultural exchange is unlimited. Pity the student who does not get to know some of these young people from other lands. Pity the professor who does not use these foreign students as cultural ambassadors in the academic community. Never has American youth had such a rich chance to broaden their world.

I was on a campus during the Advent season when the International Club was sponsoring a "Cavalcade of Christmas." Throughout the student union young men and women from lands beyond America had rows of booths decorated in keeping with Christmas customs of their homeland, depicting the traditions of their people. They sang Christmas songs in their native tongue, explained the meaning of their practices, and shared the beauty of their Nativity lore. It was like taking a tour through forty countries and one could learn in one night more than could possibly have been culled from reading a shelf full of books.

It was an adventure, bringing us closer to other cultures and bringing others closer to our own.

Some forty thousand students from foreign lands study in

American colleges every year and some ten thousand of these are here on an exchange basis.

Recently I went to Bocholt, Germany, to get the story of one of these, a high school girl from Rocky Ford, Colorado, who had gone to live in a German home. The daughter of a Protestant minister, she was living with a German Catholic family whose daughter, in turn, had come to live in Rocky Ford in the Protestant home.

These two teen-agers had exchanged parents, schools, and cultures for an academic year. Neither had ever been away from home nor did they speak the language of their adopted countries. Their adjustment, however, was phenomenal and who is to measure the contribution they will make to international understanding? In a very real way the hope for a better world lies in such programs and young people are psychologically prepared for these adventures. They are modern Marco Polos, determined to explore new approaches to old problems and discover new realms of the spirit even as the famed patrician explored the fabulous empires of his 14th century world.

The amazing thing is how many likenesses we find and how quickly our differences can be resolved, when we really get to know our neighbors around the world.

This was proved to me in the fall of 1961 when I escorted a group of Japanese religious leaders across America. They had come at my invitation; five Buddhists, four Shintoists, one Catholic, and one Protestant. I took them on a four-week tour of colleges, churches, and cities in order to familiarize them with our way of work and worship. We spent one night in a Benedictine monastery, the Abbey of Subiaco, near Fort Myers, Arkansas.

In an informal discussion, one of the Shinto leaders said to one of the Benedictine fathers, "In Japan we have great reverence for our departed ancestors. Is there anything like this in the Catholic religion?"

The Benedictine replied, "Yes, there is. We believe in the Communion of Saints; that is, we believe that some who have died are saints in heaven and can help us, and that others need further cleansing and we can help them by praying for them."

One of the Buddhists said, "In Japan we have definite days on which certain ancestors are commemorated. Do you do this also?"

"Yes," was the answer, "in Catholicism each canonized saint has a feast day on which he is honored once a year."

Listening to an hour-long exchange of views such as this, I realized how wonderful this was, especially in view of the fact that twenty years ago America and Japan were involved not in an exchange of ideas about religion, but in an exchange of the most terrifying weapons of destruction.

I remembered Pearl Harbor. I remembered standing on a hill looking down on Hiroshima and seeing how the city had literally risen from the dead. I remembered talking to people there and recalled how more than one Japanese said to me, "Do not apologize for dropping the bombs on our cities. If our country had had them we would have dropped them on you. It was war, but now we are at peace."

Now we were at peace. Now we were sitting together in a monastery realizing how small the world had become and how great our understanding needed to be. What an exciting world! What a great time to be alive!

See the World
Against the Backdrop of Time

When will we ever learn, I wondered, to project ourselves forward into time, to realize that we earthlings are all mortal immortals, that we must learn to share the earth peaceably, that our enemies may eventually become our allies and our allies our enemies, and that it is all a cycle within which we are called upon to adventure more nobly in the art of living?

I was in India shortly after the partition when unheard of atrocities were perpetrated by all parties: Hindus, Moslems, and Sikhs. I was in bombed-out Kassel, Germany, after World War II. Kassel was like Coventry in England, Coventry was like Stalingrad, and Stalingrad was like Nagasaki. In the midst of the indescribable horror of these cities, in which the rubble became the graveyard for thousands upon thousands of citizens, I could not help but think of the ironical suggestion of George Bernard Shaw, "It would be more practical for each country to bomb its own cities and let it go at that!"

That is how these things look against the backdrop of time. That is how ludicrous the events of war appear. That is how childish hatred and destruction look in retrospect. Present conflicts will seem just as unnecessary when they are viewed by future generations. Current enmities will seem quite ridiculous to future historians. But some things must be learned that cannot be taught. For, as philosopher Santayana observed, "They who will not learn from history are destined to relive it."

A New Teacher

There is a new teacher, however: our shrinking world. It warns us that no one can be victorious in a modern war. It assures us that there are no longer any secrets which can be concealed or plots that can be hidden or conquests that can be planned without every nation being aware of it. And it reminds us of a half-forgotten saying spoken by a Prophet two thousand years ago, "Blessed are the peace-makers, for they shall be called the children of God."

Know Your Neighbor

Opportunities to get acquainted with people of other cultures are not confined to college campuses. Chances are that in your own community no less than in the work in which you are engaged are people of cultural backgrounds different than your own. Instead of viewing such people with suspicion, try getting to know them. Try learning something from them. Expand your world as the world grows more compact.

I know a man, a plant foreman, whose life was suddenly complicated (so he thought) by a technical assistant who was brought in because of his scientific skill. This new man, a

Pole, foreign-trained, was having extreme difficulty with the English language, and had not yet caught on to American ways. However, the head of the plant had discovered him and had been able to vouch for him and get him to America. He considered this man a great find, but my friend, the plant foreman, found him highly disconcerting. As the enmity deepened, it appeared that an open break was inevitable.

Now it happened that my foreman friend had one consuming passion: chess. He not only belonged to a Los Angeles chess club, but he studied books on chess as a hobby. One evening he entered into an exhibition session with the chess expert, Reshevsky, who was playing some fifty challengers. My friend did not play very well against the champion, however, and he noticed that the spectators were leaving him to gather around a player at the far end of the room. Then he realized that the player seated there was none other than the assistant foreman, the Pole, and that he was giving Reshevsky a real run for his money.

My friend, conceding defeat, folded up his board and joined the gallery. Excitedly he watched. Impatiently he waited until the game was completed. The Pole did not win, but he came so close that the crowd applauded when he shook the champion's hand.

Among the first to congratulate him was my friend, the foreman, and they walked out of the hall together arm-in-arm. The common bond of chess had brought them together and they became bosom friends. More than that, their families got acquainted. Each learned about the other's customs, the women exchanged recipes, and the children learned to mix Polish and English words in a happy bilingual experiment. Laughingly, but with a serious touch, my friend said, "But for chess we would have been checkmated!"

Prepare for the "Coming of the World"

We are in the midst of a new world rich with the interrelation of cultures and ideas. Nothing can hold back this

world. No one can resist the ever-increasing need for a knowledge and understanding of other cultures and people. This does
not mean that we must lose our Americanism. It means, rather,
that our Americanism must be deepened. We are now challenged to know more about the history of our country, to be
able to trace its continuity, to recognize its greatness, and to
defend its ideals.

Certainly it is well for us to be warned about our weaknesses and to have our faults pointed out. It is only realistic
to take an inventory of ourselves and do something about it.
But the worst thing we can do is to sell America short. The
most terrible mistake we can make is to be ruled by fear of
other countries rather than by faith in our United States.

Our secret power lies not in retaliatory instruments of death,
but in compassion to mankind, brotherhood among people of
good will, security without the loss of liberty, idealism and the
will to serve. These have always been the hallmarks of American people, and the world is watching to see whether or not
we are going to lose them as our relationship with other nations
becomes more intimate.

We need, too, a growing sense of cultural give-and-take,
knowing that our strength here in America has been forged
by the contributions of men and women from every land
under the sun. They came here seeking, but they also came
with something to give.

America is just now coming into its own. It is just now recognizing its true destiny as a leader and as an exemplar in
man's quest for liberty and truth. The shrinking world, challenging us to demonstrate our worth, is exactly the opportunity
we need. And it is characteristic of us that we always rise to
our opportunity and "make it an adventure."

The shrinking world is bound to bring about better understanding among nations, for when we get to know each other
our basic motives become ever clearer, and inherent fears begin
to disappear. During a speaking tour in India, I addressed a
student group in Bombay. In the question period a student
said, "Fifty thousand CARE packages have just come from
your country. What strings are attached to these?"

I explained to him that there were no strings attached, that these shipments were the expressions of individuals and families who had no other motive but to share. It required some explanation to get this point across. My inquirer could not quite comprehend the spirit of American people. He was suspicious of us and I doubt whether he would ever have understood us at all but for this person-to-person exchange of views.

I often ask myself just why we *do* engage in some of our sharing. It is not a matter of charity, nor is it a matter of wanting something in return. It is not even a matter of trying to prove that we are basically morally good. It has something to do with an innate ethical conviction, inspired no doubt by our Judaeo-Christian heritage upon which our nation was founded, and prompted by our knowledge of the needs of others throughout the world.

We give away fabulous sums to other nations through personal, institutional, and governmental channels, and the programs have often been debated and questioned as to their intrinsic worth. Our motives *are* misunderstood, the contributions *are* frequently misdirected, the aid *is* all too often mischanneled, but we have been blessed and we have prospered though we sought no reward.

Some anthropologists believe that we are moving toward a common race in which color and cultural traits will become less distinctive, where religious denominational lines will disappear, and where political ideologies will find a common ground. A long backward look over past histories and a forward glance toward man's quest in outer space would seem to justify such a supposition. But the most significant development toward any kind of unity must happen in the "inner man." The ideal is unity not uniformity, and unity is a thing of the spirit.

As if foreseeing this, many groups and movements are emphasizing this trend. The Peace Corps itself is an expression of our awareness of our new neighborhood: the world. Years ago when a boy left home to try to make his career in a city it was looked upon as a great adventure. Mom wept and farewells were scenes of sorrow. Dad went to the railroad station

with his courageous son and patted him reassuringly on the
shoulder or else the family stood in the front yard while their
fortune-seeking yearling drove off in his Model T Ford. Home-
sickness was a household word and the breaking of family ties
a major catastrophe. All of this went out with the passing of
the front porch, the parlor, and the Model T itself. The world
became a neighborhood, and "make it an adventure" took on
a broader meaning. Hence, the Peace Corps speaks of Tan-
ganyika, Kwangju, Managua, and Penang, as if they were as
nearby as Chicago, Cleveland, New Orleans, or Seattle, and
they are.

At Pikesville near Baltimore is a center called Koinonia,
which means "fellowship." Inspired by Dr. Frank Laubach,
the great apostle of literacy, Koinonia is dedicated to equipping
people for a new kind of service in areas of world need. Its
plus factor lies in the awareness that human beings everywhere
in this old world are spiritual beings and that those who serve
must be spiritually oriented. Men no longer dare go into
foreign lands without knowing what the people in those lands
believe, what they live by, what their hopes and aspirations
are, what their language, their customs, their food, their ways
of life are like. Koinonia believes that an individual must be
able to stand in the other fellow's place, that he must be aware,
alert, alive to both the need and resources of the people he
seeks to serve.

The Fact of the Matter

Since the world is now a neighborhood we find it a great
deal more measurable than it was in days of old. The earth,
our home, has a diameter of only 7,918 miles, a circumference
of only 24,902 miles, and a total land area of only 55,885,000
square miles. Nearly three times as much of its surface, 141,-
055,400 square miles, is water. Its lowest depth, the Emden
Deep just off the Philippines in the Pacific, is 35,400 feet; its
highest point, Mt. Everest in Nepal, is 29,141 feet. The highest
temperature ever recorded, in Libya, Africa, in 1922, was 136

degrees Fahrenheit; the lowest, in Siberia, in 1892, was 90 degrees below zero. The earth's population, exploding at the rate of one birth every twelve seconds, is well over three billion; the population per square mile is about 45 persons.

This is our earth, revolving in its orbit around the sun at a speed of 66,700 miles per hour and rotating on its axis at more than 1000 miles per hour. This is our earth, said to be at least two billion years old and having nourished human life for at least half that long. This is our world: eight continents, 3,000,000,000 people, some 2500 ethnic languages, 400 religions, and with no more new frontiers to be explored excepting outer space and the inner man. This is your neighborhood!

Your neighborhood is no longer merely your home town, your state, or your nation; it is the world. Silk from Siam (Thailand) is no longer a rarity; it is a product which, like any other product anywhere in this shrinking world, is only a few hours away.

Primitive man is no longer as primitive as he once seemed. Research has shown that many of his practices and rites are deeply rooted in some universal consciousness not fully understood by people of other cultures. "Foreigner" is already a strange-sounding word, a misnomer, for in a world as small as ours there are no longer any foreigners, outcastes, or unknowns. Even the references to "good people" and "bad people" are being re-examined in the light of ultimate ends, and to determine who is "wise" and who is "unwise" also requires a definite reappraisal.

Deeper roots in the American Way are what we Americans need, together with a world view that will make us one with our fellow men around the globe. Every nation is the center of the earth. Every man stands at the heart of the universe. Every one of us is of profound importance in the ultimate destiny of our whirling world.

As this world becomes smaller, we must, indeed, all become bigger in mind and spirit than we ever were before!

Make it an adventure!

8

How courteous can you be?

A Japanese legend says that when the gods peopled the islands of Japan, they warned their created beings to be kind and courteous to one another because these paradisical isles constituted the only land of its kind in the world. The lesson was clear: in order to live together, the inhabitants had to get along together. If they could not get along together, they would probably all perish in the sea.

Today this injunction of the mythological gods may well be heeded by thoughtful men no matter where they live. So congested are conditions on the planet earth that there is no place to park, no place to hide, and hardly a place to walk without stepping on your neighbor's toes. Crowded streets, crowded beaches, crowded highways make it clear that we must become adventurers in courtesy in order to maintain a suitable place to live.

But how courteous can we be?

Houses in new sub-divisions stand wall to wall. The privacy which people once demanded is at a premium or has disappeared altogether. It was easier being courteous when we had more room.

Fenced-in yards separate families into pent-up enclosures. A home is often a walled-in citadel surrounded by other citadels whose inhabitants are literally strangers to one another. Great estates are being sub-divided; rural land which once was free is being zoned for shopping centers. Mountains are being leveled, valleys filled, groves and orchards uprooted to make way for people whose ambition is to possess a few feet of earth. It was easier being courteous when there was place to roam.

When land is unavailable, people buy apartments, and, in lieu of a permanent residence, the mobile home continues to be a symbol of the dilemma and conscience of our age. One builder in Southern California, where 1000 people per day are migrating from colder regions, said to me, "There is only one way to go—up!" So restrictions on the height of buildings have been lifted, and steel and stone are rising thirty stories to change the skyline of the great West Coast. The Tower of Babel had nothing on modern man's frenzy to find a place where he can make himself secure.

How courteous can we be in these surroundings?

To make things easier in this connection, a sudden new approach has burst over America: retirement cities. This new "concept in courteous living" is based on the idea that the elderly who have "made good" have the right to live exactly as they wish, in a model community, under sunny skies, with amiable neighbors, with ample recreational, cultural, and artistic opportunities, and within the range of the average budget. The promoters of these areas guarantee that you can own your home and trust your friends and live like a lord without worry or concern.

Retirement cities are billed as "adventures in paradise." They are advertised as "Country Club Cities for Happy People 52 Years of Age or Older." They are referred to by their founders as towns with two things missing: strangers and loneliness. The folders say that this is the "completely happy, new way of life filled with the richness of warm friendships, the sharing of the good things of life, the fun of getting together for pot luck suppers, square dances, picnics, and parties." To all of which are added "constructive pursuits in the many services and welfare activities of the community."

It remains to be seen whether this is the answer to the dream of one great segment of our population and whether out of it will come a new symphonic theme for the contented life. Is it possible that some of these citizens in these new retirement cities will grow lonely for the sound of children and the roar of traffic, to say nothing of the sight of young couples tucked away in cars on lover's lane?

It is not only homes and cities that are needed for security these days, there is also a clamor for shelters underground, a cave or cavern where, if we must, we can find some sort of refuge from the storm of war. If war should come—how courteous can we be? Should we have machine guns mounted on these shelters and, if so, what happens when neighbor begins shooting neighbor? There is talk now about "shelter ethics"— rules of conduct to be followed while we barricade ourselves. Whom shall we keep out and whom shall we let in when the threat of sudden death streaks down from the skies?

There are a variety of opinions. Some say that any country which resorts to the use of nuclear arms will have no qualms about initiating other equally merciless weaponry, and that if a man does survive a nuclear holocaust he will crawl out of his cave only to die a more agonizing death at the mercy of chemical and biological executioners. Any nuclear attack, it is said, will open Pandora's box and turn the world into a lethal chamber from which there is no escape.

Others ask what kind of a world it will be even if peace should come after the nuclear scourge. Would we not have to live continually in fear? Would the pulverizing power of an atomic attack leave anyone psychologically fit to rule? In the light of such possibilities, "courtesy" becomes a word as seemingly impoverished as gentlemanliness, an anachronistic word far too prosaic for the times in which we live. Yet, until another planet is readied for our habitation, there is, as the gods said of Japan, no other land of its kind to which we can go.

Beginning Our Adventure in Courtesy

So what do we do?

For one thing we must make it an adventure in our social

relationships and we must begin with courtesy. Though the threat of the devastating power of modern war may make our day-by-day attempt at courtesy seem futile, there is another aspect to be considered. Wars are the extensions of men's minds and moods. It should, therefore, be possible to stop a war before it starts by changing the mind and the mood of the perpetrators. We can experiment in this area in the little private "wars" that may be brewing in our own area of social responsibilities.

To do this we must recognize that individuals are as different in their temperaments as they are different in physical appearances. We cannot approach each person in the same way or with the same technique. It is vitally important that we develop a new sensitivity in our understanding of each individual.

A short time ago we went through a period of "togetherness." The word was on every tongue and we were urged to be chummy and sociable at any cost. The fact of the matter was that some people were not inclined by nature to *be* chummy. It was not togetherness they wanted, but privacy. All the emphasis on togetherness only irritated them or made them schizophrenic. But for an enforced courtesy they could easily have triggered a private war all because of this lust for togetherness!

I recall in this connection a speaker who suggested to a high school assembly that the students would do well to greet each other by saying, "Peace!" instead of "Hello" or "How y' doin'?" The speaker felt that the psychological impact of "Peace! Peace!" as a salutation would have a marvelous pacifying effect. The school superintendent wrote him three days later saying, "If these kids don't stop saying 'Peace' we're going to have a war on our hands!"

After "togetherness" we were subjected to a cycle in which the key word was "the image." Everyone from kids to corporations were supposed to create an image. President Kennedy in his rocking chair was an image of Lincolniana Americanism. The compact car created the image of sophistication. Barry Goldwater was the image of a staunch conservatism. A certain brand of whisky was the image of distinction. The short skirt was somehow supposed to be an image of national prosperity.

The trouble with all this was that a contrived image was rarely undergirded by true facts and we began to suffer both as individuals and as a nation by our creation of a facade behind which our lives went on unaltered, lives which were quite as harassed as the lives of people elsewhere in the world. We held up an image of courtesy, too, but when visitors from other lands came to our shores or we went to theirs, the image all too often proved untrue.

But here and there people started an adventure—in courtesy —determined that if a new world was to begin, it would have to begin with them in their own social relations. I found these people in many communities, separately and in groups, seeking to close the gap between the courtesy they professed and the courtesy they were willing to practice.

Courtesy on the Highway

Some of this adventuring started where it is desperately needed: on the highway. Statistics reported that 80 out of every 100 drivers involved in accidents were guilty of violating one or more traffic rules. Thirty percent had been speeding, thirty percent had been drinking, eighty percent of all accidents happened on a straight road. With these facts in mind, it was agreed that only a change in driving habits could bring down the toll, and the only way these habits could be changed was by the observance of a courtesy code.

At a retreat in California it was suggested that the highways be made a testing ground for courtesy and some retreatants went so far as to say that only a religious consciousness could ever help us behave like human beings behind the wheel. In other words, the consensus was that the only real safeguard against violence on the highway was a spiritual approach involving respect for life and proper regard for the law.

To effect this change it was pointed out that a number of interesting techniques have been developed by individuals and groups of various religious persuasions. For example, some drivers are taking seriously a small card which they fix to the

visor or the instrument panel of their automobile. The card
says:

> This is God's car. God's hand is at the wheel. God's law of
> order and right is manifest in all its mechanism. God's wis-
> dom inspires in the driver alertness, good judgment, and
> quick decision. God's patience gives this driver temperance
> and courtesy on the road.

Medals of St. Christopher (patron saint of travelers), minia-
ture figures of other saints and tiny safe-driving medallions are
being widely used to remind Roman Catholic car owners to
reflect a Christian conduct on the road. Non-Catholics, too,
are using such reminders. Drivers starting on cross-country
trips often begin their journeys with prayers for safety and
guidance along the way.

A minister at this inter-religious gathering in California described a technique he had observed in an *ashram* (spiritual
center) in Pondicherry, India. Here students were given an
impressive object lesson in automobiles. As the various parts
of the car were explained, the students were made to realize
that the intricate automotive mechanism is inter-related within
itself and with the world around it. They were taught that
every driver and every pedestrian as well as every other car
are linked together in a divine plan. They were told about
their responsibility to the car and were challenged to treat it
with self-controlled, self-respecting judgment, and were urged
to look upon their job behind the wheel as an assignment in
courtesy.

One thing was certain, everyone agreed that driving a car
requires firm personal discipline. It was also a case of, "We
have tried everything else to make our driving safer, let's try
decency." The conclusion was that those who conscientiously
employ courtesy discover that this attitude takes some of the
bite out of the annoyances that confront every driver, because
driving now becomes an adventure in self development. It was
reaffirmed that the car is a good place to begin this adventure
because some of us spend as much time in our automobiles as
we do in our homes. Courtesy, voluntarily imposed, may be the

secret that will eventually make our highways truly safe. In driving we are dealing not with a commodity, but with an idea.

How courteous can you be?

Courtesy in the Home

What is the best time for a husband and a wife to quarrel?

This intriguing question was recently discussed at a young "Mr. & Mrs. Club" in a Congregational Church. It was no longer a matter of, "Is it necessary for a husband and a wife to quarrel?" or "Why should a husband and a wife quarrel?" It was taken for granted that quarrels are inevitable, and no doubt there is a great deal of truth in such an assumption. We are all human, as the saying goes, and I doubt whether any couple would want to be spared a good, healthy squabble once-in-awhile. It may be nature's way of clearing the atmosphere, provided that it does not reach hurricane proportions. There is more than a little truth in the complaint of the young wife who, when asked why she quarreled with her husband, said, "He always agrees with me."

So the question was, "What is the best time for a husband and a wife to quarrel?" The first noteworthy answer was, "When both are relaxed!" This happy thought was supplemented by suggestions on how to effect relaxation, such as counting to ten (or ten hundred), agreeing to a stated time for the cooling-off period, separate walks around the block, or cold showers!

The second answer was perhaps more realistic. "Anytime when the children aren't around!" It was considered essentially courteous to do the quarreling in private, not in public, and certainly not in the presence of one's children or relatives.

A third suggestion which was debated at considerable length was the advice that quarrels should be held over the telephone. The volunteer for this approach testified that one time he stomped out of the house after a furious quarrel and when he got to the office he continued it via the private phone. After he had slammed the receiver on the hook, the sound brought him to his senses. He said he felt just as if he had struck his

wife! He called her up again and apologized only to find that
she had slammed down her receiver, too, and felt as remorseful
as he. So they kissed over the phone and made up.

There were all sorts of suggestions and a good deal was said
in jest, but the underlying note was that husbands and wives
should develop a courteous technique both as to time and
place when they can talk things over and in this way forestall
many an oncoming storm. The leader of the group then reviewed some of the findings of "experts," particularly those reported by the unique Conciliation Court of Los Angeles
County, which is a marriage counseling service under the
leadership of Judge Roger Alton Pfaff.

Reviewing the fact that two people living under the same
roof, joined together intimately in marriage, having loved each
other sufficiently to get married in the first place, should reach
a point where they find they are unable to communicate with
each other, the court suggested seven hints for a frank and a
friendly discussion.

1. Determine to discuss the issue as dispassionately as
possible, preferably in the evening, after dinner, when
both parties have had an opportunity to unwind from
the pressures of the day.

2. The heart of any productive discussion is consideration of the other person's point of view. This requires
thoughtful and sincere listening, which implies a desire
to understand and respect the other person's feelings and
opinions.

3. Even though the parties earnestly desire to resolve
their differences the discussion may commence to become
acrimonious. When this happens, the discussion should
be terminated and never allowed to degenerate into an
argument or an attack.

4. An agreement should be reached for a continuation
of the discussion at a definite future time when tempers
have cooled.

5. An important prerequisite to any such discussion
should be an understanding and agreement between the

parties that a lack of communication and failure to talk things over has been a major contributing factor to their marital difficulties.

6. Both parties should promise to exert every effort to create or restore friendly avenues of communication with each other.

7. Above all else a husband and a wife should never forget a fundamental and psychological truth, which is that no one has yet ever measured the beneficial results obtained from two significant and compelling words, "I'm sorry."

It occurred to me that all of these points could be summed up in a single, solitary phrase, "Make it an adventure!" An adventure in courtesy. An adventure in understanding. For unless each party is willing to approach the negotiations in such a spirit, very little will be accomplished. Who will be the first to admit, "I'm sorry?" These are very little words, but rest assured there must be a big personality behind them or they will never be spoken.

Who will be the first to give in or to be willing to negotiate? Who, in moments of family tension, will be brave enough to recall the days of love and romance and try to return somehow to the spirit of that period? Only that person will ever take such a step who is courageous enough to "make it an adventure."

The Price of Courtesy

It may not be a question of how courteous can we be, but, rather, how courteous *must* we be? For life takes on a new and richer meaning when we put ourselves in a courteous frame of mind. Every thinking person experiences a sense of self-reproach when he is needlessly discourteous. We know we could have done better and should have done better and often we would give a great deal to have a chance to relive the experience again. We may not be able to relive it, but if we profit from the lesson we have at least salvaged the better part.

Many people are discourteous because they feel that everyone else is discourteous. They would like to be different, but they question whether others would appreciate it. The truth is that the "others" feel exactly the same way, and each is afraid of making the start or of being the first to open the door —to courtesy.

An impasse of this kind is the bane not only of individual lives but extends itself into national and cultural attitudes as well. All of which is by way of saying that we are actually better individuals than we permit ourselves to be and very likely we are more benevolent and courteous as a group than we will ever allow ourselves to demonstrate.

I once asked a class of students to list the discourteous acts which annoyed them most. They said:

1. I hate most of all to have someone blow smoke in my face.
2. People who push their way in ahead of me.
3. Cars that cut in ahead of me on the road.
4. Men who don't hold the door open.
5. Clerks who ignore you.
6. Clerks who try to press an unwanted article on you.
7. Rude waitresses.
8. Rude taxi drivers.
9. Unruly children.
10. Boisterous teen-agers.
11. People who interrupt or monopolize the conversation.
12. People who are insensitive to your feelings or moods.
13. People who break promises.
14. People who cough needlessly in the theatre.
15. People who treat me patronizingly.

Of Courtesy to Children

If a child is to attain physical, mental, and spiritual stature for today's world, he will need:

1. The love and active interest of each parent.
2. A harmonious home.

3. Good examples in his moral and spiritual development.
4. Firm discipline.
5. Proper guidance in his relationship with others.
6. Fair treatment and object lessons in courtesy.

Obedience through fear is short-lived. The child will out-
grow the fear or will lose respect for the one who inspires fear.
In correcting a child, remember that it is not that the child is
bad, but rather what he has done that is bad. What he will
remember longest and what will influence him most is courtesy.

You Never Know the Influence
of Your Life on Other Lives

When I heard the report that violinist Fritz Kreisler had died,
I turned off the car radio over which the news had come and
drove along in thoughtful silence. Kreisler had deeply influ-
enced my life. He had been one of my greatest inspirations, yet
he never knew it.

I met him just once and heard him play in the days when
my boyhood ambition was to be a violinist. Awkwardly I
waited for him after a concert in Milwaukee, Wisconsin, and
when he shook my hand I was sure that there could never be
a virtuoso greater than Fritz Kreisler. More than that, I was
persuaded it would be difficult to find a gentler man as far as
sympathy and sensitivity were concerned.

His life was reflected in his playing. His concerts were as
much a testimony to his personality as to his art. Once he gave
up his musical career to study medicine. At another time he
was wounded while fighting in the Austrian army and was left
for dead on the battlefield. A comrade risked his life to drag
Kreisler to safety and the violinist often said that he lived
only because of the courage of his fellowman. He became a
convert to Roman Catholicism and a citizen of the United
States, but people everywhere were his spiritual companions
and every nation was his home.

I never succeeded in making a career out of my enthusiasm
for the violin, but the influence of Kreisler gave me a deeper

feeling for music and a richer appreciation for the quality of a true artist. Did he know how greatly he would be missed? Probably not, but, then, neither do you and I realize how much we, in our little worlds, influence and change those whose lives we touch, and how we will be missed by those who love us.

"Life," Emerson once said, "is never so short but that there is always time enough for courtesy."

How courteous can you be?

9

Make people happy!

Happiness is essentially a state of mind. It is found in a word spoken at just the right time, in a deed that is done, in a thought translated into action. It is man's highest expression of freedom, the one thing that can truly save both humanity and man. Happiness is one quality for which the individual is responsible and for which he will be held accountable at the last day. For happiness is harmony with life, and when enough people believe in it enough to live it, then and only then will we have a world at peace and an era of good will.

The best way to discover happiness is to make it an adventure, and the place to start is with yourself. By an act of will, you can be happy or sad, gay or morose, joyful or depressed. Happiness is under your control, for though you may not be able to change conditions, you can change your outlook and your approach in meeting these conditions. Happiness or the lack of it is up to you.

Start with Yourself
by Way of Others

Making other people happy is the best way to experience happiness for yourself. This is an approach we too often overlook.

A friend of mine makes it a practice every Monday morning to write a note of appreciation to someone who has done something outstanding and to send a letter of condolence to someone who has suffered loss. This requires less than an hour of his time, but the influence of his act is immeasurable and the effect upon his own life has been a rich reward. Life has become so hurried and impersonal in the world around us that a simple word of recognition or remembrance has a magical effect.

In my work as a public speaker I count it a rich reward when people comment on what was said. Listeners' impressions are the bonuses that add happiness to every public performance. I remember particularly a man who, in shaking hands with me after a program, said, "I am happy to be living in your time." That made me happy, too. At another time a woman remarked, "I came here tonight troubled and distressed. You gave me just what I needed in the way of understanding." That was a happy reward. On another occasion a listener had the charm to say, "Let me touch the hand of one who touched my heart." These comments required little time but imparted great happiness to me.

You can make yourself happy or unhappy by the way you respond to conditions or react to situations. If you resent the fact that someone owns a bigger house or a better car than you do, you block the channel that can bring you the joy of such possessions.

One of the happiest women I know has been the victim of some bad breaks in life. She has lost some of her prized possessions and might well be jealous of others whose lives have been more fortunate than her own. Instead, she blesses what others have and shares the joy they share. People enjoy having her around. She has a favorite saying whenever someone escorts her through an estate or shows her things which she cannot herself afford. She says, "I am spiritual possessor of all that I see."

Make it an adventure! Carry in your heart a friendliness for the world even though it may seem friendless. Look upon others as cooperating with you for your ultimate good, even though they may seem to be working against you. Hold to the thought that people are on your side even though their ways at times may not seem to be your ways. Persuade yourself to believe that the world is basically good and that those whose lives are intimately related to yours have been put there by a wise destiny.

Happiness Was Made to Be Shared

When were you happiest? What are your happiest moments? Are they not those times when someone else is involved in the experience with you?

Happiness means association. Mental, physical, emotional, spiritual association, and in all of these another party is always intimately involved. Though he may not admit it, the scholar would be quite unhappy alone. He must have his colleagues. The sportsman must have his opponents and his competition. The lover must have a lover to love. The writer his readers. The actor his audience. The salesman his clients. The spiritual seeker must have an object for his affection in order to be truly happy.

You may say, "I am happy when I am alone," but that is only because you know that someone else's life is intimately bound up with yours and that your "lonely thoughts" will bring that person nearer you.

My happiest moments are those in which I feel I am creating something, writing something, generating new ideas. All my life I have been trying to invent something and I have several patents on certain gadgets, none of which ever proved to be remunerative or worthwhile, but the happiness involved in the attempt was ample reward. There was the coin-sorting machine I invented when, as a boy, I worked in my uncle's bank. I spent every spare moment in my home workshop confident that I had the making of a revolutionary idea. Finally it was finished and patented. At exactly that time a company in the east came out with a device that not only sorted coins but counted and wrapped them in one swift operation. I had been several months too late, but I doubt whether anyone could have matched the happiness I had in *thinking* that I was a great inventor!

Later I had the idea for a self-lighting cigarette. A chemist at the University of Iowa agreed with me that it was a marvelous invention and together we worked out the details. Together we went to the Monsanto Company in St. Louis, and my happiness knew no bounds when one of the officials said he felt this would revolutionize the cigarette industry. First, however, it was necessary to search the patent records to see whether anything like this had ever been patented before. It had. Sixteen times! I was years too late with that, but, as the chemist said, "Wasn't it fun!"

Hobbies are fun. Sports are fun. Creative thinking is fun. The world is rich in happiness for every man who is willing to be happy. But say what you will, there is always someone else involved even when you contend, "I am happy when I am alone," or "I am happiest when I work by myself." Someone you love or someone who loves you is intricately involved in whatever you are doing. That is how it was with me in my "inventions." There were always those who were pulling for me and sharing my excitement with me and this was my deepest source of happiness. Satisfaction is something you may get alone, but happiness is always a corporate job.

The husband puttering in his workshop is happier if he knows that his wife is somewhere nearby and if he can summon her by saying, "Come and take a look at this!" The lonely fisherman I met on the Inland Sea in Japan confided to me that his biggest thrill was when he came home at evening time and his family gathered to see what luck he had that day. The Basque sheepherder spending his all-alone weeks in the mountains, admitted that his happiest hour was when the supply jeep dropped around to see him once each week. Any moutaineer will tell you that it is tremendously satisfying to stand on a peak alone, but to stand there with a companion is the perfect joy.

You want to be alone? Of course you do. Everyone does at times. But happiness lies in knowing that your being alone is not a lifelong solitary confinement.

That is why when I hear people say, "I would be supremely happy if I could just get away from it all," I want to tell them that true happiness cannot be found in a social vacuum or fully experienced in a tightly insulated life. Happiness involves the feeling of being wanted and needed. It involves the knowledge that another life is intimately bound up with your own. Like love, of which it is a part, happiness needs companionship, for it is this that gives life meaning and purpose.

Often on trips abroad I meet people who are traveling alone. They are not only alone, they are usually lonely. They see the same sights and hear the same sounds and walk the same paths as others do, but because there is no one with whom to share their felings, their happiness is limited. I experienced this just recently when on a flight over the Pacific I saw the breath-taking beauty of the setting sun. During these moments I wished with all my heart that someone near and dear to me might have been at my side, and it seemed to me that joy is only partial joy when it is experienced alone, and beauty is only half beauty when it is unshared. And, yet, others in the plane were also thrilled at the sight and the thought came to me that the joy and beauty *were* being shared and that an overpowering happiness, beyond the reach of words, had for the moment caught our hearts.

Make People Happy

You make people happy when you see life through their eyes, when you admire the things they treasure, when you try to understand their dreams.

You make people happy when you are forgiving and, through forgiveness, happiness comes to you. You can also bring happiness to yourself by forgiving yourself for things foolishly or thoughtlessly done. The Scriptures have a sound psychological approach to this when they say, "Happy is he who condemneth not himself." (Romans 14:22). As we make ourselves miserable by self-reproof, so we cause others mental suffering by reproving them. When we learn to forgive both ourselves and others we restore happiness to its rightful place in these all-too-brief years of mortal life.

You make people happy and bring happiness to yourself when you do unexpected acts of kindness without fanfare and without thought of reward. "People in need," says a Greek proverb, "are the ambassadors of the gods." That is to say, opportunities for doing good bring out the best in us when we do good deeds, and the chance for making another life happy should not be overlooked.

It is, of course, a highly critical business, this matter of doing things for others, and a great deal of wisdom must be employed in the doing. How far shall we go in helping a man without spoiling the chance for him to help himself? How long is the second mile? How forgiving shall we be in view of the scriptural injunction to forgive seven times seventy? We must exercise great judgment, but if we remember that selfless happiness in us is reflected in true happiness in another, we have some sort of standard by which to proceed. Someone once said, "If happiness hears her name pronounced, it endangers her existence."

Most of all you make people happy when you praise them. Even if you wish to criticize someone, always praise him first. Let him know you are on his side and that the suggestions you are making are made with as much honesty and insight as possible. Make him feel you have his welfare at heart, that you admire his ability, that you are able to put yourself in his place.

Happiness Is a Habit

I often hear people say, "I would like to be happy, but I can't. I have too much on my mind. I am too involved. Life has become much too complex."

This is a strange complaint. Turn it around and ask, "What do you plan to do? Keep on being *unhappy?*"

Everyone knows that discontent and worry about life's complexities can mold themselves into a habit. Now let us learn that happiness can be a habit, too. It is simply a question of

where you wish to direct your mind. It is most of all a matter
of deciding in which field you are willing to make it an adventure: in the field of happiness or discontent.

One thing is sure, without happiness we walk in darkness
and things will go from bad to worse. With a happy outlook
and a will to change, we can compel ourselves to walk in the
light. The "light" touch is what we need.

Our greatest mistake is that we lose sight of life's positive
alternatives. When you are poor, affirm that poverty need not
be your constant lot. When you are sick, recognize that health
can be your heritage. When you are dejected, tell yourself that
this is but an interlude and not your destiny. When you have
bad breaks, insist that good breaks are in the making. Given
time, these thought forms become habitual and assume reality;
and, as we have said, happiness can be a habit, too.

Happiness is always waiting for the true adventurer. He can
see it in the face of a child, hear it in the laughter of youth,
feel it in the clasp of a hand, even taste it in a meal with a
friend!

Take an inventory of what you *have*, not of what you lack,
and you will see how much you have to be thankful for. Compare yourself, for a moment, not with those who have more
than you, but with those who have less. Now compare yourself
with those who have more than you and realize what you, too,
may have as you face your world anew. Happiness, as has
often been said, is an inside job. It can become a habit.

> You can think twice as clearly if you are happy.
> You can do twice as much work if you are happy.
> You will get twice as much out of life if you are happy.
> You will be better liked if you are happy.
> You will have better luck if you are happy.
> You will even live longer if you are happy.
> So why not be happy?

10

Techniques for daily living

The Bible has a parable about the use of talents which applies equally well to the use of techniques; the gist of it is that a talent buried is useless and a talent put to work is productive. This is true whether in the use of money, time, or life.

Judaism has a saying, "A man's existence has three periods: the period when his body develops, the period when his thought develops, and the period when his deeds develop." In our consideration of deeds we are now ready for techniques, and one of the first is the use of affirmations.

Affirmations are word-power statements, commands to the subconscious mind, ordering it to do your highest bidding, and helping you immeasurably in circumstances which may seemingly be beyond control. The reminder, "Make it an adventure!" is in itself a most wonderful affirmation. Remembering it, you will analyze situations honestly, think them through seriously, and meet them courageously. The words remind you to look for the best, to believe in the best, and to expect the best. This is how so-called "miracles" happen, and they can happen to you.

Metaphysical Gadgets

The other day I visited with Lowell Fillmore of the Unity School in Lee's Summit, Missouri. Here is a man in his eighties who sets an example of health and happiness for men half his age. He is an indefatigable worker, is at his desk at seven every morning, is rarely if ever ill, and I doubt whether anyone has ever seen him out of sorts! How does he do it? First of all, he makes life an adventure with himself and with all the world around.

As the originator of what he calls "metaphysical gadgets," Mr. Fillmore has introduced some usable techniques which have tremendous power. His metaphysical gadgets are affirmations designed to meet specific situations which confront each of us in our day-by-day associations. The idea is to memorize these "gadgets" and to call them into play when neded. For example, if you must do something you do not want to do, but know that you should do, something you have been putting off and which has become more difficult because of postponement; instead of fighting it any longer, fortify yourself to meet it with the affirmation, "*I go to meet my good!*"

You may not be completely sure that it is going to be your good, but you affirm it just the same. Metaphysically, it is a proven fact that if you believingly assert an affirmation over and over, an actual power is generated which helps produce the desired result.

Now you might ask, "Could I not just as easily say, '*I go to meet my bad?*'" Metaphysically, you could not, because the law seems to work only in your highest *good*. It is a bit like hypnotism. You will not, under hypnosis, perform any act lower than your moral code allows, and you will always do best on your highest moral level. This law of hypnotism is also a law of life.

So you say, "*I go to meet my good!*" And as you walk to your appointment or to your rendezvous with whatever you have overly-long deferred, you keep saying, "*I go to meet my good!*" When you stand face-to-face with whatever you must encounter, you continue to affirm, "*I go to meet my good!*" And good begins to answer your summons.

It does not even matter at first whether you really believe the statement to be absolutely true. As long as it is on the level of your highest consciousness, and if you persistently affirm it,

you will find that the goal is gradually realized. It is well to remember that there are ways of *doing* even when there are not
always ways of *knowing*. It is a technique and it works most
wonderfully in one's relationship with others.

"I go to meet my good!"

Try it when the doorbell rings or when a neighbor calls you
over unexpectedly or when a friend telephones to say, "I just
happen to be in town, come and join me for a moment."
Though he may be the last person you wish to see or if you
feel that this was the one moment you wanted to get away all
by yourself, for the sake of an experiment just this once, make
it an adventure!

I once used one of Mr. Fillmore's metaphysical gadgets with
great profit. He has one which says, "No one cometh unto me
save the Father hath sent him." This is especially good for adjusting yourself to people who drop in on you only to waste
your time. The technique is to listen to them with new understanding and to see them through new eyes. Not an easy assignment, to be sure, but one well worth trying.

I tried it with a retired missionary who used to visit us with
annoying regularity. Not only did he stay to dinner, he spent
weekends at our home and, what was worse, he had a habit of
repeating his reminiscences of life among the Eskimos until I
knew his anecdotes by heart. His most monotonous one went
like this: "After the long Arctic night when it was time for the
sun to return, I would take my cornet and climb a hill. At the
psychological moment I blew a bugle call and up came the
sun!"

So weary was I of hearing this story of the human chanti-
cleer that I began to make excuses to be away whenever he
dropped around. One day I was caught, so I made up my mind
to make it an adventure, doggedly saying in my heart, "No one
cometh unto me save the Father hath sent him!"

As soon as the missionary had settled himself comfortably
in his chair, he began, "Did I ever tell you how, after the long
Arctic night, when it was time for the sun to return, I would
take my cornet——"

Once more the scene unfolded, but this time as I listened I

said to myself, "What if he had miscalculated the time for the sun's return? What if he had blown his bugle call and the sun had *not* come back?"

Amused and fascinated by this idea, I wrote a play about it, called it *Sunrise by Request*, and sold it for a thousand dollars. All because of a metaphysical gadget and the will to make it an adventure!

Life Is a Laboratory

We are now close to the operational method of affirmations. You see, the power lies in affirming a higher good than that which seemingly exists, and in *willing* better results than would ordinarily seem apparent. In a complex situation, you seek to discern the perfect solution. In trouble, you hold to the belief that the difficulty can be perfectly overcome. In the midst of strife, you visualize peace; in the midst of anger, tranquility; in the midst of sickness, you seek to see yourself whole and well and affirm this condition as confidently as though the goal had already been achieved.

The reason this involves you and the world is because public opinion is against this kind of reasoning. Almost anyone will remind you that it is unrealistic, if not infantile, to say that all is well when you can plainly see that all is *not* well. True enough, your physical eyes and your common sense may persuade you beyond the shadow of a doubt that all is not well, but you also have an inner eye and an *uncommon* sense which sees beyond the apparent, which reaches beyond the known, and which goes so far as to never say die even when confronted by death. It is with this uncommon, supranormal sense that we are here concerned.

Every last one of the great philosophers has told us that things are not what they seem. Every last one of the great scientists has assured us that there are worlds within worlds. And every famous metaphysician has insisted that our conditions, our surroundings, and our world are fashioned by the thoughts we think and the way we think them.

Yet, only a minority of people believe this, and if you profess to believe it and live it, you will find yourself part of the
minority. So this is not the kind of approach to life that you
proclaim from the housetop. On the contrary, it is a technique
with which you adventure quietly in the laboratory of your
own experience, valiantly pursuing it if you have the courage
and the will, even when it does not seem immediately to prove
itself according to your wish.

What actually happens is that we *do* see things as they exist
around us, but at the same time we also see them as they exist
in the ideal world. We recognize that poverty is real, but we
affirm that abundance, as the inevitable law of substance, is
also real. We recognize sickness, but we recognize even more
that nature's law is the law of health. All of this, of course, is
an exercise in faith. It is a technique in the art of living. But
most of all, it is an adventure!

Begin with the Morning

When you begin a new day, give yourself an affirmation
along with your morning cup of coffee. Affirm something like
this: *Today is a new opportunity. I wipe the slate clean of all
that is past. I start this day confident that all things will work
together for good.*
Even the person most adept at the use of techniques often
finds himself hard put to maintain this complete confidence
throughout the day unless he keeps the affirmation alive as the
day progresses, keeps it alive by remembrance and repetition.
Users of word-power statements will tell you that it is best to
memorize them and repeat them word for word, and that re-
calling the spirit of them works a magical power.
I remember a visit to a Zen temple near Tokyo, Japan. Here,
where men learn the art of tranquility and adjustment to life,
I was shown the meditation room where each retreatant prepares himself for his day's activities by sitting for an hour in
motionless silence. When, later in the day, I went into Tokyo
with one of the men and realized how he maintained his calm

in the midst of the whir of this largest city in the world, I asked him his secret. He said, "I never leave my place of meditation."

He meant of course, that even though he was *here* in Tokyo traffic, he was also *there*, there in his meditation room where, so far as his spirit was concerned, he saw himself tranquil and reposed. It seemed to me a wonderful and usable technique: remember your place of mooring. When life gets in a tangle and your world gets full of knots, you are where you are, but your mind remembers the morning affirmation when quietly and calmly you affirmed that all things would work together for good. You re-affirm this now and reawaken the power, and the oftener this is done the easier and more effective it becomes.

You Are in Command

You can take your troubles to your psychiatrist, your doctor, your minister, your friends, even to the one who loves you most, and the best anyone can do for you is to awaken the power in you which is already there waiting for you to recognize it and to command it to be used.

Most situations always present us with an alternative, certainly always a mental alternative. If, for example, we are delayed in meeting an appointment or if time schedules have suddenly become confused, we can be mastered by them or attempt to master them. We have a mental choice. The equivalent or counterpart of mental distress is mental calm. We can effect this calm by affirming, *Nothing happens without meaning and good will come even out of this.* This is not denying that the tangled situation exists; it is a matter of rising above it with the greatest confidence of which we are capable. Another affirmation often used at such times is: *I am always in the right place at the right time!*

Until I began my research in this field, I had no idea how many people used this word-power technique, for as has been said, this is not the kind of practice which the user publicizes. It is, rather, a personal adventure between himself and his particular world, and it is concerned with him and his specific need.

I know individuals who have developed exceptional poise and ease in meeting people by preparing themselves for the meeting through the use of the affirmation: *It was divinely ordered that we should meet.* This may be the kind of statement that belongs only in a lyric and that is sung about without any idea of taking it seriously. But where it is taken seriously it works wonders, especially for those who are willing to make it an adventure.

The next time you are introduced to someone, try holding a statement of this kind and see for yourself what happens in your attitude toward the person. If you are fearful or worried about an appointment or if you do not have "good vibrations" about a person, mentally affirm: *It was divinely ordered that we should meet.* Or, when you meet someone who does not seem to respond to your good intentions, quietly hold to the affirmation, *I believe you feel the good thoughts I hold for you.*

When the world seems dark, you can change things by having the courage to mentally declare: *I see my world as a place of beauty, opportunity, and light.* Believe it. Visualize it. Many a person has found his way through periods of indecision and mental depression by affirming: *I am now perfectly directed in the thoughts I think, in the moves I make, and all is well.* There are many who, when starting on a trip, confidently declare: *The spirit of God goes before me making safe, happy, and successful my way.*

It is an adventure and those who embark on it are the best to judge what it does to them as they employ these usable techniques in the world in which they live.

Sometimes a Miracle

I would be the last to put a limit on the power of the adventurous life. People are always doing things which I thought could not be done, going to places which I thought could never be reached, and finding things I thought could never be found.

Sometimes there are miracles.

I met such a man one night at the home of a friend on the
West Coast. He was a slender, middle-aged, scholarly man with
rimless glasses. We had been talking about life's unexplored
and unexplained dimensions when he told me his remarkable
story.

At sixteen he had been blinded, the result of an accident,
and subsequently he had been provided with a seeing eye dog.
The dog, Saga, became the light of his life. The dog acted as
his eyes when he went to college, and when he got his degree,
Saga was on the platform with him.

Some years after graduation he and Saga were walking one
night on a New York street near his home. Suddenly he heard
the terrifying screech of brakes and the onrush of a careening
car. The dog was jerked out of his hands. Then he heard people
scream. Frantically he searched about him, only to discover
that Saga lay dead at his feet.

He said he stood there knowing that part of his world had
been destroyed, feeling rather than hearing the voices of the
people around him. A policeman asked him for information. He
replied but he hardly knew what he was saying. Then he heard
someone whisper to him, "Come, I will take you home."

"Dazed and confused," he related, "I took the dog in my
arms and let the stranger take me to my apartment. He went
in with me. We wrapped up the body of the dog and after a
moment the stranger asked, 'Do you mind if we kneel and pray
together?' I said to him that this was about all there was left
to do, and got down on my knees.

"I never heard a prayer so full of power. He was so confident
about the presence of God that even when he prayed for the
return of my sight, I believed him. I remember how I gripped
his hand before he left. Then I went to bed and tried to sleep.
In the morning when I awoke, I saw light streaming in through
the window. I saw things I had never seen before. I saw the
wrapped body of Saga. I saw my room. I was afraid to believe
it. I dressed and hurried into the apartment across the hall, cry-
ing, 'I can see! I can see!'"

Later he went to the police station. He reported that he was
the man whose dog had been killed, the blind man. The officer

called several members of his staff and asked him to repeat what had happened. They wanted everything in great detail. Then a policeman said, "There is just one thing wrong with your story. No one took you home. There was no stranger with you. You insisted on going to your apartment by yourself and we watched you go. There was no stranger."

But to him, even now as he told me the story, the stranger was real. *Someone had been with him.* The fact that he could see was also real and it was real to me. And I thought as I looked at him and listened to him that, perhaps, if we but had the faith to adventure and believe, nothing would be impossible.

The Power of the Unseen

That, too, is a technique: to believe in the power of the unseen. And that is why in my research in the life and belief of people around the world, I never consider any of their practices strange or curious. Whatever they do has meaning for them, and the more I remember this fact the greater my orientation with the world becomes.

I used to be curious about the cultures of other people in the early days of my research; now I am interested. I used to judge their beliefs against what I had been taught to believe; now I judge them against their own convictions. I used to be hesitant to share my deepest feelings, thinking they were meaningful only to me; now I have learned that deep experiences are universal and the common heritage of every man.

Everyone is moved by an unseen power and to him who believes it, it is real. Only he who sees the invisible can do the impossible. It is a technique to live in the unseen as well as the seen. Remembering this and making life an adventure have persuaded me that there are, therefore, no natural enemies as men used to believe. Changing circumstances often bring even the most incompatible people together and in the long reach of history there is something that seems to be working out its will. All life is one life. The difference is often more in degree than in kind, and it is surely true that we are part of all that we have met.

Meet the Changing World

Live as though you were part of the world, not apart from it.

The world is always changing. No one, so far as we know, not even among the long-lived Hunzas in the Himalayas, is living now who lived a hundred and twenty years ago. An entirely new world citizenry is in charge of things and still the world goes on.

The other day an ad in a magazine caught my eye. It said, "You are older at this moment than you have ever been and you will never be as young again as you are right now!" So provocative was this reminder that I do not even remember what was being advertised. It was the kind of thought that stirred me to action and made me give my life a second look.

I used to have a terrible difficulty in accepting a changing world. I dragged along with Alexander Pope who said, "Be not the first by whom the new is tried, nor yet the last to put the old aside." There is some truth in that and surely a thing is not necessarily good just because it is new or bad just because it is ancient, but when I think of how I used to resist change, I realize I lacked the spirit of adventure.

That is what it takes to keep up-to-date: adventure and a volitional act. It needs a technique with a key phrase: *stay synchronized.* Anyway you look at it, the world keeps changing and moving and unless you stay synchronized, you will find yourself out of time. My friends in the audio-visual field have a word for it; they call it "out-of-synk" or "off-synk." Such is the case when action and sound are dissonant, when they do not mesh, when they are fighting each other; and that is what some of us do in our relationship with the changing world.

Be different, be unique, be critical of the world, and be a non-conformist if you wish, but don't be "off-synk." In an economy where eggs are 70¢ a dozen, you can waste a lot of time trying to find some at the old price of twenty-three.

The other evening I was at a party in Los Angeles where a man was bemoaning the exaggerated price of real estate in the greater Los Angeles area. "I remember," he lamented, "what that property sold for six years ago. I remember what I could have bought it for ten years ago. Look at it now!"

A man in the group spoke up. "But you didn't buy it! So forget it! What's past is past! You've got to begin with today, stupid; you can't go back!"

He was right, of course. We might wish to go back. We may even have lost something along the way, but "you can't go back," and it could be that we have gained something along the way, too. But whether we have gained or lost, we are challenged to make it an adventure as we face our changing world.

One of the surest signs of old age is when you begin to bemoan the fact that the past is past.

The Old-Young Equation

One feature that impresses me in so-called "foreign cultures" is the respect youth has for its elders. There is a relationship between youngsters and oldsters in India and the Orient which often puts our attitude in this area to shame. What is the reason and what can we do about it?

For one thing, American youth consider themselves worldly wise at an early period, and we American adults, refusing to admit that age can have charm, try to stay out of the old age bracket as long as we possibly can. Youngsters want to be oldly wise, and our elderly want to remain worldly young, and therefore things are in the shape they are in.

There are other reasons, of course: economic, social, environmental, but what is needed is a new consciousness in the matter. A person should certainly stay as young as he can as long as he can, but he should not be ashamed of the philosophy of life which the ongoing years provide as a bonus for growing old. In the Middle East, for example, not only is the familial attachment notable, but young people honor their elders because of the wisdom and knowledge they possess. Old people know the legends and the proverbs and the secrets of this life and of the life to come. They give the impression that this wisdom is a great adventure.

There is a rare subtlety involved here, for these patriarchs have learned not to be obvious about their knowledge. They do not try to foist it on the younger generation. There is always a bit of the romantic about what they know or seem to know, and just enough of the mysterious to tantalize the youth.

I was with an elderly *hadj* (one who has made his pilgrimage to Mecca) one day in Damascus. He was taking his young grandson to the great mosque. This was more than just a matter of "let's go to church;" it was the youth's introduction to a great new world to which his grandfather held the keys. The ablutions, the removing of the shoes, the kneeling postures, the words of the prayers were links in a bond that would rarely, if ever, be shattered.

Can it be that we have lost too much of our love for tradition and have we, perhaps, written off some of the deepest meaning of our national and spiritual life and thereby broken the line of communication between generations? We turn our children over to various organizations for their youth work, and to the Sunday Schools for their spiritual instruction, and to a variety of clubs for their social life; and we are in danger of professionalizing ourselves into isolated age camps unless we begin, as individuals and as families, to make life an adventure.

Viewed in terms of techniques, an interesting approach was suggested to me by a businessman friend of mine, father of three "typically American" children, eight, eleven, and thirteen, all boys. His home, he confessed, had become nothing more than a way station, and as for mealtimes when the family was together, it was, he said, a "rat race."

Then one day he and his oldest son had the rare privilege of eating with the monks at a Benedictine abbey. They were greatly impressed by the Benedictine silence during meals, broken only by the quiet voice of the reader as he read from an inspirational book.

On the way home the boy said, "Dad, why don't we try that?"

"Try what?" asked the father.

"Silence at meals," said the youngster. "We don't even pray before we eat."

The father looked at his son for a long moment. "You serious?" he asked.

"Sure, I'm serious," was the reply. "We could try it and see what happens."

Try it they did. Each meal is now introduced by a word of prayer and at the main meal of the day, one of the boys reads a portion out of an appropriate book. The father said to me, "I don't know how long it will last, but it has changed our whole family life. Whether we keep it up or not, the influence will never be forgotten. It is a great experiment."

It was also an interesting approach for a family that decided to work out a technique, as all families can, for their adventure in daily living.

11

The utopian seekers

Many people have an idea that if they could change their surroundings they would automatically improve their lives.

This may be one reason why one out of every five families in America moves every year. It may also help explain the phenomenon of why so many Americans are living on wheels. They are looking for utopia, which has come to mean the "perfect life in the perfect surroundings," or the ability to find the "garden of tomorrow" today.

Social experts have laid down many rules for rovers, in the hope of helping them find just the right location as well as actually finding themselves. "If you are thinking of moving," they say, "look at the town, not the house."

"Case the neighborhood!" is another one of their dictums.

Check the weather reports.

Rent a place for a while before settling down permanently.

Get the appraisal of competent friends.

Mingle with the people, the town and school officials, the storekeepers, the members of churches and service clubs.

Be sure you like your job in your new surroundings.

Above all, in order to get the best reactions about a new location: be friendly!

This is all very important, they say, because by changing your environment you may automatically improve your life.

What do you think?

The Search for Utopia

My mother had four children of whom I was the youngest. When I was a boy we lived in a small six-room, brick house and Mother used to say, "If we just had a big house where the kids wouldn't be under my feet all day, I am sure things would go a good deal better, and I for one would be a good deal happier."

Shortly thereafter we moved into a big twelve-room white frame house where we each had our own room and a music room and a library and a front room with a sliding door which was kept closed except when the minister came. I thought things were going very well, but a few years later Mother said, "With a house as big as this a person needs a maid. If we just had an apartment instead of all this house, I am sure everything would be better all the way around."

By this time my sister and one of my brothers had married and we moved into an apartment on the second floor, close to my father's place of business. It was a six-room apartment with a long hallway and rather attractive, I thought. But I felt I could understand my mother's complaint when, after several years, she said to my father, "This is no place to live, up here on the second floor without any ground to call our own and so close to our neighbors we can reach over and pull down their curtains. If we just had a little house, then everything would be wonderful."

Soon Mother and Dad were alone and they decided to move back into the little red brick house where we had grown up as kids. The cycle was complete, from little red brick house to little red brick house. Did my mother ever find utopia? No. She used to joke about it, saying, "Changing houses never really changed my world!"

She was making it an adventure, but in the wrong direction.

Utopia, she learned, works from the inside out. Like happiness, it is a state of mind.

Ever the Quest

I found other utopian experimenters who believed the secret lay not only in changing locations, but in changing the entire social and political system. These were collectivistic groups who came to the new world from Germany, Russia, France, and Great Britain almost as soon as our country was colonized.

Under the freedom of the American way, these experimenters built their little isolated communities and introduced their own form of government. One hundred and twenty times such groups tried to find utopia and there is no doubt that they will always be something of a legend in the dramatic history of America. Our country gave them the liberty and permission to see whether they could find a better system than that provided under the constitution.

I explored their trails from border to border and from coast to coast: the Amana Societies, the Harmonists, the Separatists, the Shakers, the Icarians, the Perfectionists, the Aurora-Bethel Communes, the Hutterites, and many others. All are in a state of decay or have vanished from the scene. They wanted to be a people apart. They set up a controlled social order which advocated a community of goods, made their people conform to a particular standard, and said, in effect, "From each according to his abilities, to each according to his needs."

They were not communists in the sense of Russian communists, but they were opposed to free enterprise, the competitive system, the right to travel, the right to criticize, the right of free association, and they pictured the "outside world" as a place of corruption and sin.

I turned up the broken stones of their abandoned altars and read their secrets. They thought they could create a better life than that which American democracy had to offer. They never found that better life, and many a frustrated utopian leader was ready to admit it. One said to me, "America is not perfect, but we made a mistake when we tried to improve it by opposing the principles of freedom on which it was founded."

Youth and Utopia

It is interesting to see how ideas have changed since the days of those who wanted to be in America but not of it. Today's youth has its own dreams of what constitutes utopia, and hundreds of these young people have shared their dreams with me as I lecture on college campuses throughout the nation. Whenever I asked a student, "What, for you, would constitute utopia?" I realize how mature their thoughts and how deep-seated and realistic is their quest.

"Having been raised in America and brought up under the American system," one says, "I have utopia. To me it means the freedoms we enjoy and the responsibility I have to maintain these freedoms."

A junior student submits, "I consider utopia as being more an awareness than a physical actuality. I consider it as being on the other side of a line, similar to the line of infinity in mathematics."

"I want a utopia," writes a coed, "where there is work to be done, work that is worthwhile from the standpoint of the benefit others will derive from its completion, work that challenges my intelligence and imagination, work that allows me to be independent from it occasionally. I want a utopia in which there is efficient production and distribution of material goods, where there is ample freedom for self-development within reasonable limits, where there is opportunity to dwell in natural surroundings of one's choice, and the privilege to be near the people that you love."

"When I think of utopia," says a graduate student, "I think of a place where man is equal to man, but where one may get ahead by fair play and honest competition. I do not believe that equality means that everyone must always stay on the same level, for it is natural and expedient for the more ambitious to get ahead. I believe that men of various races and creeds would be necessary in a utopia, for nothing could be more monotonous than sameness or more deadly than having all men compressed into one standard pattern."

"Utopia to me," says a teen-ager facetiously, "is the garden of Eden without the snake."

"To me," says a thoughtful sophomore, "utopia would be the discovery of my life's greatest purpose, for in following that purpose all confusion and disorder would end in happiness for me and for my little world."

It was spring when a college coed wrote, "Utopia for me would be a place where I could sit quietly and meditate as long as I wished and when I wished. A place where I would be surrounded by friends, true friends, but where there would be one particular, special friend, and we two could be alone if we wished to be. A place where the winds blow gently and the earth is rich. A place where I could avail myself of books and news of the outside world so that I might have something to think upon. A place where, perhaps, I could create something of my own, such as a book or treatise on civilization. This utopia would also have a place for me to fish or swim, if and when I pleased. There would be a place, too, for me to worship God in my own way and at my own pleasure. In short, a paradise on earth where I could pursue the desires I have learned to love in the outside world and still remain aloof from the cares and worries of that world." To this, she added, "P.S. Upon rereading this, it sounds a little selfish."

A young man, re-entering school after a period of military service, said, "If it were possible to set up a dream world of perfection, I doubt if I could remain enthusiastic in such a society. In my opinion man would lose his searching, questing, scientific mind and grow content to put forth just enough effort to eat, exist, and carry on a very monotonous life. I have had the opportunity to observe several forms of government during the past few years and I firmly believe that our democratic way of life is the best utopia for me. To imply that our society *is* a utopia is a misconception. However, here we have the chance of making one if any man ever had the chance."

Then there was the political science major who said, "My

utopia would concern itself with the freedom of the individual, that greatest gift of the founders of America. I see my country as a government whose highest aim must always be to further individual freedom, yet also to care for the liberty and welfare of the group as a whole. I see my country as economically secure, where all workers will receive the fruits of their labor and the means by which they earn the right to call themselves laborers, whether it be tilling the soil or guiding a brush across a piece of canvas or, with skillful mind, planning the construction of a new scientific achievement. I see my country as a place where a group of people, regardless of color or creed, may live together in harmony, recognizing that each has a right to be what he is. I see utopia based on the Constitution of our United States in which the individual is perfected, for we cannot live in a perfect society if we ourselves are imperfect or if we cease to pay respect to the documents that made our country great. That is how I see it, with a closer connection between our government and our Creator, for it is only through some Higher Power that we build and mold a morally sound existence and dare to dream of utopia."

"In my utopia," a graduating senior concluded, "there must be individuals whose personalities are blended with those of the group. There must be universal education and voluntary obedience to law. There must also be conditions conducive to health, opportunity, religion, and peace of mind. Most of all, I must recognize that I have a part in bringing this utopia into being, for helping to work for it will help me to find it."

Utopia and You

In most of the student papers, utopia was related in some way to our democratic way of life. In all of the papers, it was implied that unless something happened within the individual himself, utopia would be unattainable. This proved to me how far the world has come in its realistic approach to a better life.

Young people believe in utopia as a reality even though they know that the word *utopia*, first used by Sir Thomas More in 1515, referred to an imaginary isle. In fact, another name for utopia has always been *nowhere land.*

Nowhere land it may be. An imaginary isle may be its best description, but let us believe that whatever is conceivable is also attainable, to a degree, at least.

Should you stop loving because you do not find perfect love; or cease the search for perfect health or perfect friends or perfect weather just because you have not yet found them? There is always one great clue: make it an adventure! But adventure in the right area. Adventure in your highest ideal.

When does life seem most worthwhile? Whenever it is, treat it as something precious. Be grateful for it and let it make a better person of you.

Where does life seem most worthwhile? If at a certain location, absorb the spirit of it and go back to it, in memory if not in person, when you need its inspiration.

Who makes life most worthwhile? Carry the affection of that person with you and feel his understanding and companionship and remember that while reality never quite fits the dream, you can always recall the ideal!

What makes life most worthwhile? If it is during moments of acclaim or triumph or when someone appreciates you or when you do something for others, let the remembrance sustain you in moments when you feel you are not appreciated or when you do something and are completely misunderstood.

By all means, if you know what makes life most worthwhile don't overdo it. "Too much use of even good things is hurtful," says a proverb. Part of the secret of utopia is the realization that you have it, while still recognizing that having too much of it might cause you to lose even that which you have.

During my voodoo experiences in Haiti, I attended a ceremony on Christmas Eve. Part of the ritual had to do with feeding the *loa,* the invisible spirits that are supposed to rule one's life. To dramatize the feeding of these unseen entities, five girls about six years of age were ushered into the ceremonial room. They had fasted all day and now near midnight they were very hungry.

As they sat on the floor near charcoal burners, each was

given a huge calabash bowl heaped full of rice and chicken. Drums began to beat and the voices of chanting worshippers filled the room. In this setting the girls began to eat, happy and laughing. Soon they wanted to push back the bowls, for they had eaten all too fast and all too much, but they were not allowed to quit. The voodoo priest stood over them, chanting, gesturing with his hands, ordering them to, "Eat! Eat!" One girl began to cry. Another appealed to him to let her stop. When one of them screamed, the priest crouched down and fastened his hypnotic gaze upon her. The *loa*, he warned, had not been satisfied. Again the girls plunged their hands into the chicken and rice, forcing themselves to go on. The feast turned into torment. "Eat! Eat!" cried the priest. "It is not you that eats, it is the *loa!*" By now the children were hysterical, but the drums and voices drowned out their sobs until the calabashes were licked clean.

It was voodoo, but it reminded me that in the long run utopia is more dependent upon moderation than upon excess, whether in eating, in pleasures, in acclaim, in luxuries, or even in love.

Whenever, wherever, whoever, whatever it is that brings utopia to you, it will cease to be if you overdo it. True utopia may actually be made up of fragments held together by hope and joy and little moments of happiness. Perhaps it must be this way, for there is nothing less utopianesque than utopia overdone.

Your Secret World

You cannot lay down rules for utopia saying it must be this or that. It is many things. It is finding one's place in life, or one's companion in life, or one's talent or health or hope or faith. It may be "making good" in life, or loving or being loved, or seeing your children grow and hearing them tell you that they are grateful that you are you. Utopia is many things to many people, and different things for different people, all the way from the pacifist to the warrior and from the hermit to the socialite. But in all cases it seems always to involve the discovery of a little world, a microcosm, which is strictly *your* world, one in which your thoughts and hopes and loves are yours, just yours; a little world which is able to appreciate the big world but one which is also capable of absorbing and sublimating the shocks of the big world.

This is where the utopian experimenters failed. They tried to escape the reality of the big world. They also overlooked the fact that they themselves were restricting the individual within the limits of their own self-created world, the commune. The microcosm, the little world of the individual, this is where utopia begins, and its secret is an inner consciousness into which no one else should intrude. There is an inner life which is yours and yours alone. No one should rob you of it, nor should you try to rob others of their little world.

A Japanese fable says, "One day Soshi was walking on the bank of a river with a friend. 'How delightfully the fishes are enjoying themselves in the water!' exclaimed Soshi. His friend said, 'You are not a fish, how do you know that the fishes are enjoying themselves?' Soshi replied, 'You are not myself. How do you know that I do not know that the fishes are enjoying themselves?'"

Which Way Utopia?

One morning I had an appointment with a Trappist monk. On the afternoon of the same day I interviewed a prominent industrialist.

These men lived in totally different worlds. The thirty-five-year-old Trappist was dressed in the plain brown garb of a lay monk, with a cowl that could be pulled up over his shaven head. I sat with him in a cold, barren, pictureless room of the monastery. The only wall decoration was a crucifix, the only furnishings a cot and a chair. The monk's brown beard, his shuffling steps, his thin, stooped body gave him the appearance of an old man, but I shall never forget his serenity and his obvious love for Trappist life. He owned nothing, not even his clothes or his name. He never left the monastery grounds and he spent his entire existence in work and prayer, getting up at 2 A.M. to begin his day. Pledged to the vows of obedience, poverty, seclusion from the world, celibacy, and perpetual silence, he actually never spoke except in rare cases when he was given permission by the abbot or when he asked permission, which he seldom did.

I met the industrialist in his elegant suite of offices. The red leather furnishings were obviously expensive. The floor was covered with Oriental rugs. Pictures of his yacht glamorized the walls, and portraits of this man's family dominated the marble mantel of the fireplace. A picture-window looked out over the skyline of the city. This forty-year-old man, the successful president of his firm, took me in his foreign-built car to his country home, a home on a lake connecting with other lakes so that his yacht and his speed boat could be docked close at hand. In his den I saw citations from various charitable groups which acknowledged his philanthropies. His hobby, apparently, was helping people who needed help, and there was no doubt that he was spiritually motivated.

The monk and the industrialist had never met. I doubt whether the Trappist had any idea of how a wealthy man lived. The industrialist had never seen a Trappist. I doubt whether he knew how the monks lived. Yet these two men had something in common: the secret of the microcosm. Each had created a little world of his own which, for him, was the world he desired and the world in which he fulfilled his purpose.

For the Trappist, the yachts and cars and homes would have been a burden. He was too passive for such things.

For the industrialist, the life of the Trappist would have been unthinkable. He was too active for that. However, the monastery walls did not imprison the Trappist; they protected him, and he helped people by means of his prayers. The possessions of the industrialist did not imprison him. He helped people through his deeds.

They were different men, yet they were alike. Each had reached a desired goal and each had discovered his world.

They had created for themselves a kingdom of the inner self in which they ruled.

The Trappist shared with me some of the inspiration that came to him in his moments of meditation. He told me of the Presence he felt in the Matin hours, of the peace he found in his work and of the satisfaction that came to him in his vocation.

The industrialist spoke to me about answers to prayers in his life, about ideas that had come to him in the quiet of his office, or when he was involved in acts of social service.

The Trappist had his vows. The industrialist had his code of ethics. One had his sacrifices, the other his philanthropies. One his monastery, the other his church. Each had his work and each his microcosm, his little world.

I never think of a monastery without remembering the monks who have found God in the silence.

I never see an industrial plant without remembering that there are men who have found Him in activity.

Wherever you may stand, with the Trappist or with the industrialist or anywhere in between: make it an adventure!

Secrets to Live by

In one's relationship with the world and one's attempt to find integration in his world as this pertains to what we have called the utopian quest, certain secrets can be of help.

For example, if there is a condition or circumstance which you feel should rightly be yours, *don't wish it, will it!*

If there is a problem or a difficulty standing between you and your enjoyment and appreciation of life, *don't fear it, face it!*

If you are confronted by an obligation or a duty which may seem distasteful but which must be done, *don't dodge it, do it!*

If a bad break comes along or if your life becomes involved by a force seemingly beyond your control, *don't curse it, cure it!*

In any analysis of those who have come close to a thorough

companionship with life, I am convinced that these steps have contributed immeasurably to their orientation in the social scheme. I have discovered something else. People who have found their "utopias" have included three ingredients in their approach:

1. Faith to believe
2. Work to enjoy
3. Someone to love

You may wish to change the order, but the secrets remain and they are all inter-related. If you have faith to believe, you can find inner strength; if you have work to enjoy, you will find outer expression; if you have someone to love, you will always find purpose in life. Faith, work, love—and to paraphrase a well-known saying, we must also say that "the greatest of these is love."

There are, of course, bound to be times when disappointments will challenge every one of these ideals no matter how positive your thinking or how determined your philosophy. It is inevitable that questions will arise and doubts creep in no matter how you fortify yourself against them. Utopia is no guarantee that life will be without its problems, but it *is* a guarantee that you will always master the problems before they master you.

In your search for utopia or for whatever you wish to achieve—make it an adventure!

12

Your place

in the scheme of things

There is an old saying that the man who can see beyond the next payday is exceptional. If he can see into the future for five years, he is a genius; if for ten years, he is a prophet and a seer.

But no matter how limited our vision may be, one thing we are all beginning to realize is that life is a series of interlocking experiences. You are where you are and what you are at this moment because of an unbroken chain of events far more intricate than the complicated mechanism of the finest computer. Because of *that, this* happened; because of *this*, another series of events was introduced. You cannot escape the cause-and-effect process, but by recognizing it and being conscious of your responsibility to it, you can better control your future and come to terms with your place in the scheme of things.

It Can Happen to You!

Consider the case of Bashir Ahmed Sarban of Karachi. By now you may have already forgotten this dark, mustached, forty-year-old camel driver, but it was he who by virtue of nothing more than a bright, intriguing smile caught the attention of Vice-President Lyndon Johnson on a Pakistani street.

All his life Bashir Ahmed had been just an ordinary man with an extraordinary sense of his destiny. He was versed in the folklore of his people. Although illiterate, he had memorized many proverbs. Life to him was always the great adventure, even though he could as easily have bemoaned his lot. After all, what is romantic about being a camel driver?

Then came the day of the visit of the Washington official. Ahmed's smile seemed to say, "You, Mr. Vice-President, have your place in life and I have mine, and which of us is filling his position the greater, only time will tell!"

Captivated by the simple style and easy manner of the camel driver, Mr. Johnson invited him to America as his guest. Bashir Ahmed came, wearing a long black coat, white trousers, a fur cap, and his ready smile. It was winter and when he was asked whether he did not mind the sub-zero weather, Bashir Ahmed said, "It is not the cold that I feel, but the warmth of people's hearts."

He toured the Capitol like a king and crossed the nation like a potentate. He learned to write his name and to say, "Hello" and "Thank you," but mostly he spoke in Urdu and his proverbs were translated into English so that people could learn that "there is a time when every man makes an impression on the world."

Whether he was posing for his picture at the Vice-President's Washington desk, hobnobbing with the Kennedys, participating in news conferences, or flying by private plane to Mr. Johnson's ranch in Texas, Bashir Ahmed found his status increased, but he never lost his unaffected charm. When an automobile firm presented him with a blue truck to use in his homeland, Ahmed unabashedly requested that it be repainted green, the national color of Pakistan. When he wound up his coast-to-coast tour and prepared to go home, he was loaded down with gifts. Moist-eyed, he said, "Allah has been unusually good to me!"

This happened to an unknown camel driver, and who knows what will happen to anyone? Who is to say what changes a day can bring forth in *your* life? Make it an adventure, for the unexpected in some form or other *can* happen to you!

Life Gives Meaning to Life

American history is in a very real sense the history of individuals who have made their lives adventurous. As their stories reach out across time, who can appraise their influence? Who can measure the contributions of these lives, or, for that matter, the influence of yours?

Take, for example, Virginia-born Robert McCormick. Here was a dreamy-eyed farmer who throughout the period from 1780 to 1846 spent most of his time trying to invent all sorts of gadgets. His ever-active mind generated so many ideas that he "spread himself too thin." He took out patents on inventions all the way from blacksmith's bellows to a threshing machine, but nothing was ever spectacular. A sad and discouraged man at the age of sixty-six, he often wondered what influence he would leave on the world.

It happened that he had a son named Cyrus and, in the eyes of this boy, Robert McCormick was a special kind of hero. Every attempted invention was always an inspiration and an incentive to young Cyrus. In fact, before the elder McCormick died, Cyrus was already working to perfect the crude and cumbersome threshing machine which his father had designed. He started where his father left off and, driven by the spirit of his parent, he eventually gave the farming world its first and greatest mechanical "hired man," the McCormick reaper. It had many "impossible" innovations such as an automatic self-raking device, an automatic hand-binding, harvesting attachment, and mechanical fingers able to tie knots with wire or twine, something which experts had said could never be done.

Because the machines worked best in well-kept fields, farmers began improving and grooming their land. Agriculturalists contend that the McCormick reaper gave rural America its first sure step toward mechanized farming. Labor, released from farms because of this early mechanization, helped to build up industry in cities. It was now possible for America to provide more grain and sell more exports. And, for whatever it is worth, it is said that in order to distribute his machines to the widest possible market, Cyrus McCormick was responsible for introducing the first installment buying for farm machinery.

Add to all this the fact that he made enormous gifts to various schools and was responsible for McCormick Theological Seminary, to say nothing of political and social contributions, and you have some idea not only of his influence, but of that of his father who often felt that he was destined to die as an unsuccessful man, lost in obscurity.

Or take a man like John Everett Clough whose name may be as unfamiliar to you as it was to me. I heard it first in the little Iowa town of Fayette when I lectured at Upper Iowa University. I was told casually that, "This is where John Clough once went to school." Then I heard his name again in India, and the story fit together into an incredible saga of the boundless influence of one man's life.

When John Everett Clough was a student, he used to wonder what he could do to help the helpless in the world. His concern was translated into action when he became an ordained Baptist missionary. He went to Nellore, India, where one day an outcaste visited him and begged him to come to the little village of Ongole and start a church. Clough went. His congregation was made up of Madigas, a name given to the then despised tribe of untouchables who were leather workers. No one had ever wanted to help the Madigas; no Christian had ever recognized them as worth working with until Clough came, but so great was his love and so powerful was his influence that converts soon came to Ongole by the thousands.

When a famine struck south India, help for the desperate government came through Clough's Madigas. They worked, shared, and prayed. So selfless was their spirit and so great was their dedication that 10,000 Hindus asked for baptism in the Christian faith. For a little while the matter of caste and outcaste was forgotten. At last the untouchable Madigas were looked upon as human beings. Schools, mission houses, and hospitals sprang up in Ongole and Madras.

There was a Hindu who, hearing of the work at Ongole, watched earnestly from afar. How greatly he was affected by the actions and ideas of John Clough no one can say. All we know is that this Hindu had the title of "Mahatma," which means "great soul," and that his name was Gandhi. We know that he eventually became the father of a nation in which men of all castes are now challenged to live together equally as men of God.

All of this happened because a young man on a college campus did more than wonder about his place in the world; he made it an adventure!

Your Influence and You

Your influence for good or ill is always greater than you realize. It extends further than you realize. It changes life and the world more than you realize.

I was asked one night to speak to a group of students on a college campus. When I got to the classroom on this stormy evening, there were only seven young men in attendance. I wondered whether we should have a meeting at all or whether we should go out for coffee and call off any formal presentation. Then I decided that since this group had made a special effort to come out on a bad night, these seven were as important as seventy or seven hundred.

They *were* important because in the group was a graduate student who was making an important career decision on this particular evening. By virtue of my remarks, he went into foreign service and later made an unusual contribution to our government's relationship with Saudi Arabia.

We are continually extending our influence. The structure of life makes our participation in the lives of others inevitable. The very word "living" implies association with others. No man liveth unto himself, as the saying has it, and no one can possibly go through life without radically affecting the course of his fellowmen. In fact, the discovery of self is not always discernible within ourselves but is often found by noting our influence in the lives of others.

Take the case of Sally who lives somewhere in Oklahoma. I heard about Sally one day while visiting the Los Angeles Meals for Millions Foundation which supplies multi-purpose food free to needy people all over the world. "Food-for-freedom" is its motto and it gets its support from donors from many walks of life. Sally is one of them. For more than ten years this anonymous woman has been sending almost daily letters to Meals for Millions, notes written on scraps of smoothed-out paper, but always inside, carefully wrapped, is a nickel or a dime or a quarter, or when times are bad, a few pennies. Sometimes the envelopes are homemade and smell of flour paste. Usually there is postage due, but there is always the appealing, laboriously handwritten line which says, "Yours in Christ, Sally."

For a time, Meals for Millions tried to return these little contributions, realizing that Sally no doubt needed the coins as badly as refugees needed food. These protests were emphatically overruled. She insisted she had enough to eat, a roof over her head, and that this was her way of saying "thank you" to God and life. "Yours in Christ, Sally."

Lately she has sent an occasional dollar. It may be that things are going better for her, that the housework and the ironing and the baby-sitting are picking up. Meals for Millions said, "In thirteen years of this giving-from-the-heart out of material poverty, this woman has given $982.77 or, to put it another way, she has provided enough multi-purpose food to feed 32,759 people hungrier than she."

"Yours in Christ, Sally."

Character Is Still the Measure of a Man

Some do not believe it, but it is true just the same. In the long run, character is still the criterion against which your

place in life is measured. Time will erode everything but that:
the real you.

You have a place, a far greater place than you realize, in
your relationship with the world. You have a chance, a bigger
chance than anyone knows, to play the part for which you are
specifically equipped. You have an opportunity to go as far
as you wish in your relationship with the life of your time,
especially if you are willing *now* to make it an adventure in
the realm of character.

Evidence of this was impressed upon me when I read that
Pope John XXIII proclaimed a lowly Peruvian to be a saint
of the Roman Catholic Church. Now it may be that very
few people aspire to sainthood, and there is a good chance that
the Peruvian Martin de Porres never gave it a thought. Nonetheless, he is now sainted, and more than 30,000 people
gathered in Vatican Square to hear his life praised by Pope
John as an example of the kind of character the world still
needs.

The reason I was interested in this event was because some
years ago I stopped at the Blessed Martin Cafe in Keokuk,
Iowa. It was a small, friendly place crowded with guests, and
on the wall was a statue of Martin de Porres.

"Is this restaurant connected with the Roman Catholic
Church?" I asked the waitress.

"No," she said, "We're Protestants."

"Is it sponsored by a religious organization?"

"No," she replied. "Oh, you mean because of him?" She
indicated the statue. "That's Brother Martin."

Then she gave me a little booklet entitled, *Meet Brother
Martin,* which I read while waiting to be served. This told
the story of how Martin de Porres, patron of social justice,
was born in Lima, Peru, in 1579 and of how he lived until
1639. His formula for the good life was extremely simple: he
was interested in the needs of others and tried to see what
he could do to fulfill those needs. In later life he became known
as the "saint with a broom" because he was always doing
menial jobs like sweeping, mopping, cutting hair, and other

common tasks. His most dedicated work was helping the poor and the sick and, most of all, he was instrumental in founding homes for crippled and abandoned children. Once when he was told that it was too much for him to care for so many homeless, he replied, "Well, then, I will just have to multiply myself."

So his influence traveled from Lima, Peru, to Keokuk, Iowa. Recognition of his life came to Keokuk in 1948 when a Negro physician, Dr. William Harper, decided that it would be like Brother Martin to have a restaurant where school children could be served at cost and where needy people could, if necessary, be served free.

Now, because of the canonization, I realized that the influence of this "saint with a broom" had lighted fires of faith all over the world and that is why cardinals, priests, and people came to Rome, and why thousands in Lima marched through the streets chanting and praying and remembering the character of Martin de Porres and wanting, no doubt, to live a little better and make life more of an adventure because of him.

Widen Your World

You widen your world when you make it an adventure in your relationship with other people. When you do this, you realize you have unlimited potentials which were never discovered because you were never called upon to use them.

One of the most successful businessmen I know told me one of his secrets. He said, "Make a new acquaintance every day." He started this technique twenty years ago when he first came to town. A stranger, having no special connections to recommend him, he had come to start an insurance agency. He made it a point to meet at least one new person every day, to learn and remember the name, and to find out something about this individual's interests. He made it a game, an adventure, in never forgetting this person. Whenever he saw him, he greeted him by name and showed a cordial interest.

All this time he was not trying to "sell insurance" or even advertise his agency. He was simply building good will and the day came when all this paid off. Soon everyone in the area knew him and he knew everyone and today he is unquestionably a success.

You widen your world whenever you learn people's names, when you memorize the streets of your city, when you learn something about the history of the local scene. You widen your world without ever leaving Hometown, U.S.A., simply by exhausting the information about the town and its people. The bigness of your world does not always depend on what you own, but on what you *know*. It is judged not so much by what you say, but by what you *do*.

I am always meeting people who inspire me to be a better person. Occasionally they even make me feel there is an undiscovered greatness in me much like that which I see in them. I am never quite the same, for a while, at least, after being with these people and even when the spell of their presence wears off, I still find myself trying to figure out what it is that makes them great.

What is it they have in common? Not wealth, because some of them are far from wealthy. Not college degrees, for many of them are truly self-made men. Not family tradition or background, because we rarely discuss this. The quality they have in common is an unselfish *interest in the other fellow*. They make me feel they have an interest in me and in my work without intruding and without seeking anything for themselves. They have the canny sense of knowing what is going on in the other person's mind, bringing out hidden thoughts, hidden energies, hidden talents, and hidden dreams. They have a way of triggering the best in me, the best which I may even have forgotten I had, and that is what makes them unforgettable.

In short, they widen your world and inspire you to make it an adventure.

People sometimes tell me that I bring out the best in them, too. They say I am interested in their beliefs, their hopes, their struggles. That is true. You cannot make life adventurous within yourself without wanting to touch the adventurous spirit of others. You cannot love without being loved, or share ideas without having ideas shared with you, or be forgiving without having other people forgive you. The wider your world, the more you will widen another's world as well.

Speaking of forgiveness, it has always seemed to me that everyone should be allowed to make at least one big mistake in his life and be forgiven for it. The Good Book says something about forgiving seven times seventy, but this may be beyond the limit of human charity!

Of course, there are degrees of error and sometimes *one* mistake *can* be fatal. But I am thinking in terms of lapses in judgment, moral weaknesses in conduct, and the like. If a person is honest enough and big enough to admit his mistake and if he is determined to profit by it, he should by right be exonerated. Your place in the scheme of things demands that you forgive and that you be forgiven.

Reality, as we all know, never quite fits the dream. There is always a gap between the goal and the striving, and often it is our strong hope for realization and fulfillment that causes us to err and come short of the mark. It has been said, "The life of every man is a diary in which he hopes to write one story but writes another; his humblest moment is when he compares the volume as it is with the one he hoped to write."

We humans are all bound together by invisible but nonetheless very real ties. The common experiences of life bind us together: such things as suffering, sorrow, sickness, pain, joy, success, triumph, and love. We widen our world when we realize the universality of these experiences. Mystery also unites us, the mystery of life and death, of the unknown, the unconquered, the unexplored. Expectation unites us, the expectation of things to come and of new experiences yet to unfold.

The culture of a people should not be judged as if its object were to develop a certain type of system or a standardized type of industry or a specific form of art or even an undisputed political form; all these are by-products of the main aim of every culture which is to build or express a form of life through each individual in his own specific way.

You widen your world every time you open a book, every time you catch the thought of another person, every time you detach yourself from a preconceived theory, every time you interest yourself in a new subject, meet a new friend, examine a new object, or contemplate a new idea. Never in the history of man has the wealth of nations been within the reach of every individual as it is today when science has opened so many hidden doors, when exploration in both the cosmos and in consciousness has presented man with so many excitingly new horizons. These worlds are yours to explore, to enjoy, and to contribute to with whatever you have to give.

The Gist of the Matter

Believing as I do, that my life's purpose is to interpret for myself and others the things people live by so that we may all learn how we ourselves may live better, I must point out that I have found no single individual who has ever fully comprehended all of life. No modern man has satisfactorily explained the meaning of either extreme pain or absolute joy. No one has ever solved the riddle of the universe which, as Schweitzer said, creates while it destroys and destroys while it creates.

But one thing I have surely learned: the best adjusted and the most vital individual is he who keeps his spirit, mind, and being alive with the adventurous quest.

How is this done?

It is done by relating your life to all life, by recognizing that there is always an unrealized potential sufficient to meet all needs in the world around you.

It is done by meeting the world as it is, without bitterness though it may have hurt you, without resentment though it may have frustrated you, without vengeance though it may seemingly have turned against you.

It is done by being confident without being arrogant, by being successful without letting success become a fetish, and by making good without losing your sense of goodness. In all of this, make it an adventure as you realize your place in the scheme of things.

Then, too, there is the matter of faith and to this we now turn as we consider the *spiritual adventure* in your life and mine.

PART THREE

The Spiritual Adventure

13

Life-changing ideas

We come now to the most challenging encounter of all. By far the oldest in human history, it is always dramatic and fascinatingly new. We call it the spiritual adventure.

Harry Emerson Fosdick once remarked that this adventure is first of all a "personalized, psychological experience." No doubt it is, for its deepest meaning is found in what it does to individuals. We can talk about religion changing the world, but we always come back to the question of how it changes *us*. Our own personalized, psychological experience is something we can most easily and quickly understand. Thus it has always been.

Religion goes back to the very beginning of human history. Long before the first crude altar evolved into a temple, or before the worship of gods assumed the high proportion of a holy faith, man was trying to come to terms with the Unknown. The phenomenon of birth intrigued him, the moods of nature enthralled him, the mystery of death frightened him, and, to put a stamp of sacredness on these untoward forces, he fashioned elaborate rituals and sacrifices, hoping thereby also to influence and appease the power of the Unseen and make himself more secure in the mysterious universe which was his home.

Dreams fascinated him. When he dreamed he imagined that

his "spirit self" left his body and wandered into strange and distant places while his other self kept silent watch. The crossing of the paths of dreams and death gave him his first vague glimpse of immortality. Death became another form of sleep and ancient man buried personal belongings in the grave along with the body, possessions which the sojourning spirit self would need as it continued on its uncharted way.

We moderns feel that we have solved many of the old mysteries, others we have boldly discounted; but religion for us is still the great personal adventure, a process of search and discovery. We believe that true religion is a life-changer and a life-discoverer. If all this old world needed was a different social order, we could turn the problem over to the sociologists, or if it needed a new economic system we could call in the economists; if a new psychology of life could save us we might enlist the psychologists, or if a new political approach would solve our difficulties we could turn things over to the lawyers or the politicians. But our dilemma calls for changed individuals and that is why we need spiritual adventuring and a new look at the life-changing ideas that have come down to us by way of the living religions of mankind.

There is a good chance that what we need are not only new ideas, but a new dedication to old ideas that have long been advocated but never sufficiently tried.

Consider the Idea
That God Is Good

Here is a concept as old as Christianity, one that is persistently repeated from every pulpit in the Christian world, is professed by almost everyone, but lived by scarcely no one.

What do you think? Do you believe that God is really good? We profess it, of course, but do we truly believe it? And, do you really believe that God is a happy God?

An aunt of mine, a chronic invalid, put it this way, "I just can't imagine God being happy, the way things are in the world!"

Now a "happy God" may not be exactly synonymous with a "good God," but the relationship is very close. If we really believed that God is good, that He actually wished to bless us and watch over us and cause things to work together for *good*, our attitude and outlook on life would be considerably happier and more hopeful than it is. Is it possible that we still fear God as much as the ancients did and that we are just as superstitious and fear-ridden as they were? Not that we should bring God down to a hedonistic level or humanize Him, but neither should we ascribe to Him less goodness and less happiness than we ourselves are capable of experiencing.

For one full day, make it an adventure by actually living in the belief that God is good and see for yourself what happens to your life. Recognize His goodness in the weather whatever the weather, in people whoever the people, in your destiny wherever your destiny may lead you. Just for today affirm that "God is good." Look at situations as though they had divine meaning. Meet your problems as if they were meant to help not hinder you. Visualize God as a good friend who is on your side.

Too many of us have a feeling of guilt when life is good. Why? Do we feel we do not deserve it? Are we concerned because others may be less fortunate than we? Why not accept our goodness and our blessings and use them to help and bless others and be happy in the doing of it.

My research has taken me into all sorts of religious services, formal and informal, liturgical and popular, but no matter what they are, they all seek to postulate that God is good. All try in some way to persuade their people that God is love, that He loves us, and that we have abundant blessings for which to be grateful.

I remember my first visits to Pentecostal services where people shouted, "Halleluiah!" and "Praise the Lord!" At first this enthusiasm shocked my orthodox sensibility, but after a time I not only got used to it, I realized that these people wanted to tell the world that God is good. They carried this "glory message" into prisons, sick rooms and into slums where you would never imagine that people would ever believe that

God is good; but they did believe it and I saw the spiritual adventure being born in strange and unlikely places.

Late one night in Milwaukee, Wisconsin, I boarded a street car and found myself to be the only passenger. Up front the motorman gazed out at the nearly deserted streets. Gradually I realized that he was quietly singing a catchy gospel song. I walked up to where he sat. "Pardon me," I said, "do you belong to the church on 14th and Brown?" "Praise the Lord!" he exclaimed, "how did you guess?" "By the happy way you sang," I told him. At this, he seized my hand. "Praise the Lord," he repeated, "we have a happy God!"

I have been in churches of many faiths where the minister greets his congregation with a friendly, "Good morning!" as he steps into the pulpit. I have heard the congregation respond with a similar greeting and everyone seemed in an immediate awareness that the God they had come to worship was a friendly God.

In answer to the minister's question, "How is everyone?" the worshipers replied, "I am well, happy, and prosperous in spirit, body, and mind."

I have gone to churches where the minister prepares his people for meditation by saying, "Be comfortably relaxed. Put aside all worry and concern. Feel the spirit of God moving in you and through you during these moments with love and joy."

To be sure, religion is a serious matter, but there is something contradictory if we fail to give it a light and practical touch, for that is how we live our lives. Why should we put God into a morbid category when we are constantly trying to escape from morbidity? Some people say, "Now, I've got to be religious," as though they were entering a dark cave and had no idea what ghosts might be lurking in the shadows. The true adventurer in faith makes *all* of life his laboratory and does not believe in fragmentation.

I met a minister in St. Petersburg who had a wire-haired terrier. I asked, "How did you ever train your dog to be so well mannered?" "It was not difficult," the minister told me. "Whenever he did something he wasn't supposed to, instead of scolding him, I said, 'You are God's little dog, and God's little dog is gentle and kind.' So he just naturally got to be gentle and kind."

Which reminded me of the prayer of that great spiritual adventurer, Francis of Assisi, who said, "Dear Father, hear and bless thy beasts and singing birds, and guard with gentle tenderness, small things that have no words."

Saints instinctively seemed to know that God is good. And so do children, which may be one reason why they "sat in the lap of the Lord" and why He said, "You must become like one of these."

This brings to mind a Protestant minister who has the habit of wearing an ecclesiastical collar and is therefore often mistaken for a Catholic priest. One day two youngsters fighting in an alley came bowling out into the street just as the minister was passing. Sheepishly one of the boys said, "Will you forgive us and bless us, please, father?" The minister said, "Yes, come here and I will bless you." They came and stood before him as he spoke a quiet prayer. After he had finished, one of the boys said, "You aren't a real father or you'd have had us kneel." "Sure he's a real father," the other declared, "didn't he bless us instead of bawling us out?"

Bless and scold not! That is quite an approach to life. "He who thinks of good," says a proverb, "must think of God, for God is good."

So say the spiritual adventurers as they turn from what could be toil and drudgery and find, as they find all of life, a personalized, psychological experience.

It is not new ideas we need, but old life-changing ideas which have all too rarely been tried. Such an idea is the one we have been talking about, the idea that God is good and that He is a God not averse to happiness.

Make Him your adventure!

And Take the Golden Rule

The Golden Rule is another very old idea. Some say it is the oldest and profoundest ethical statement ever uttered by man.

It is found in all of the great religions of the world. Practically every child in every faith everywhere on earth has learned it or heard of it. The Christian faith puts it into its most popular form and rightly attributes it to Jesus who, in His Sermon on the Mount, said, "Whatsoever you would that others would do to you, do you also unto them."

I am continually meeting people who insist that we need no other religious text than this one found in Matthew 7:12. They say it embodies a complete philosophy of life and that if it were put into practice we would automatically have a world at peace.

Even youngsters believe in it. I was listening to a Salvation Army band in Chicago one night and when the lassie with the tambourine came around, a boy standing next to me gave her a dollar bill. I said to him, "What is your religion?" He said, "I don't have any. All I believe in is George Washington, Abraham Lincoln, and the Golden Rule."

Life-changing words! "Whatsoever you would that others would do to you, do you also unto them." Edwin Markham said, "We have committed them to memory, now let us commit them to life."

But how to do it? And why don't we do it?

Some say, "We don't do it because there is nothing in it for us."

But there is everything in it for us. That is the great secret of every religious practice, Christian and non-Christian alike; there is always something in it for us. In every spiritual idea there is something in it for the spiritual adventurer: a new vision, a new life, a new law of reward, a new outlook, a new world.

Obviously there is just one thing to do with this old life-changing Golden Rule: make it an adventure! If everyone waits until the other fellow does it, and if everyone waits until his neighbor does it, no one will ever do it.

Who is to begin? The spiritual adventurer. If he really wants to put the Golden Rule into operation, the challenge is squarely up to him.

Every thinking person eventually comes face to face with

this situation. Every honest explorer in the field of faith reaches a point at which he must ask himself the honest question, "How can the world be changed unless I change?"

A Lesson from the Orient

I met a man in Japan who once had been a member of the Diet. For many years he was instrumental in making laws and seeking to enforce laws, and his philosophy was: "Until mankind can be trusted, there must be laws and penalties."

Then one day he asked himself, "But who is mankind?" It dawned upon him that he, most of all, was part of mankind and that he could not by any stretch of the imagination stand outside the circle, for even though he was a law-maker, he was often a law-breaker. In what way, he wondered, was he different from other men just because he talked a good brand of legislation and dared stand apart and point an accusing finger at "mankind?"

So he went to a temple, a Buddhist temple, and stayed there for three days and nights meditating and reading holy books. Versed in the Shinto, Buddhist, and even Confucianist faith, he now read and re-read the Sermon on the Mount in the New Testament. What impressed him most was the Golden Rule.

Now, of course, he had heard the Golden Rule many times. Confucius, before the Christian era, had told his followers, "What you do not want done to yourself, do not do to others." Buddhism had its Golden Rule which said, "Do not do those things which will cause others trouble. As you would not harm yourself, do not harm others." Shinto had always said in effect, "Treat others as they themselves would wish to be treated." But it was the saying of Jesus which seemed to captivate the mind of this Japanese legislator. He could not rid himself of the Galilean's challenge and if anyone was to "do unto others as you would have others do unto you," he ought, by rights, to be the one to do the doing!

After three days of prayer and soul-searching, he decided

to commit to life what he had committed to memory. Resigning from the Diet, he moved to an abandoned house near Kyoto where he began a life of service and selflessness which eventually attracted a community of followers numbering more than two hundred.

Through more than forty years the influence of this man, Tenko Nishida, has changed the thinking of politicians, industrialists, and Japanese of many walks of life. Almost anyone in the Kyoto-Yamashina area can tell you about Tenko-san. So unique is his impact upon people that he is rapidly becoming a legend, all because he got hold of an old life-changing idea and made it a modern adventure.

This does not mean that everyone must change his job or give up his career in order to change his life. The greatest test of the Golden Rule is to live it in our day-by-day operations where we are, with what we have, and among those we work with here and now. Our present place in life may be the very best and the most logical place to put this life-changing idea into practice.

The better world will come about only when islands of "changed individuals" have been created—a worker on his job, an employer in his office, a scientist in his laboratory, a farmer, a businessman, a housekeeper, a teacher, a minister. Get enough little worlds of changed individuals and we will soon have a big changed world.

Take the Old Idea
of Being a Co-worker with God

A salesman friend of mine was troubled. He had an uncanny ability to sell, to over-sell in fact, and his high-handed techniques were beginning to bother him. Some salesmen are worried because of failure; this one was worried because of success. He knew that he was clever, all too clever sometimes. He said to me, "A man can easily get lost in the rush of things and be defeated by his own enthusiasm to put over a deal."

What bothered him most was that his basic Christian belief was at conflict with his practices. He had a motto on his desk, a very good motto, that said:

> If you are true to number one, God;
> And to number two, your fellowman;
> And to number three, the company for which you work:
> You need never worry about number four—*you*.

He had the motto, but he was not living that way, and he began asking himself what it actually meant to be true to number one, God. Certainly it meant being a co-worker with God, and if this was true, he felt a growing need for some stabilizing force in his life. How could he make this his adventure?

One day, on St. Valentine's Day to be exact, his wife gave him a tiny cross to put in his lapel. He began wearing it. When he made his sales calls and sometimes during moments when he was tempted to push hard to put a deal across, he quietly and inconspicuously touched the cross as if to calm himself and reflect on what he was doing.

"I began to notice," he confided to me, "that the cross was like a rudder fixing my course and keeping me in tow. It regulated my thinking. I began to feel a deepening sense of service and responsibility to God, to my fellowman, to my company and to myself. In other words, the cross put meaning and spark into the motto I had always had on my desk."

This idea of co-working with God is an old idea. It goes back at least a thousand years before the Christian era when Hebrew prophets looked to God as the architect of a new order, an order in which man's deeds reflected God's wishes, and man's acts were supposed to be in harmony with God's designs. It goes back to the Persian prophet Zoroaster who once told his people that God needs help, that there were powers of darkness seeking to thwart God's work in the world, and that those who shared God's ecstasy must also share God's concern. Most of all, it goes back to the Christian faith and to the Man who walked by the Galilean lakeside urging men to "Follow Me."

Co-working with God
Is a Workable Idea

Co-working with God is one of the most workable, life-changing ideas you can possibly find. It is apparent everywhere; in everything you do, in everything you say, you can find partnership with God a great directive for your life.

As I was writing this there was a rap at the door. The man who had been trimming the hedge along my driveway wanted me to inspect his job. "It looks better than it did before I came," he said with pride. It surely did. He had worked with nature in bringing out a greater beauty. Then he had to tell me his favorite story, the old story about the new minister who stopped to praise his parishioner's garden. "It looks as if the Lord and you have done a most wonderful job," the minister said. "Yes," agreed the parishioner, "you should have seen the mess it was in when the Lord had it all alone."

No one, it seems to me, ever stated the idea of partnership with God more beautifully than did the late Alan Stockdale:

> When God made the earth,
> He could have finished it, but He didn't;
> He left it as raw material to tantalize us,
> To start us thinking and experimenting
> And risking and adventuring,
> And therein lies life's greatest meaning.
>
> God gave us an unfinished world
> So that we might share with Him
> The joy and satisfaction of creation.

These words made a profound impression upon me when I first heard them. Great light seemed to leap out from these thoughts. Somehow this idea of my being a co-worker with God had escaped me throughout my youth and had eluded me during the days of my religious training.

A partner with God in "the joy and satisfaction of creation!" It was a most wonderful approach to an integrated life, and the more I thought about it the more I realized that every last one of us has a specific talent which God can use in His continuing work of creation.

Who is to say whose talent is the most significant? Constantine the Great, who was converted to Christianity by seeing a luminous cross in the sky, made his imprint by converting an empire. This was a great thing, but a lowly, unnamed widow who cast a coin into the temple treasury during the days of Christ, was recognized by the Master as a mighty great person, too. She was a co-worker in her way no less than Constantine was in his.

"God gave us an unfinished world so that we might share with Him in the joy of perfect, finished things."

In Dr. Stockdale's words I found a strong talking point with which to answer students who often asked, "What's the purpose of my life anyway? Why am I here? Where should I invest my career?" I could now tell them that where their particular talent best met the need of the world was where God wanted them to be.

I understood now better what Emerson meant when he said, "Self-trust is the first secret of success, the belief that your being here means that the authorities of the universe *put* you here, and for a cause, or with some task strictly appointed . . . and as long as you work at that you are well and successful."

Co-workers with God! It was an old and ever-new adventurous thought!

Then Dr. Stockdale went on to tell us that God left the oil in the rock, the aluminum in the clay, the lightning in the clouds, and reminded us that these things would still be there, unused and undeveloped, had not man taken up the challenge and put his mind and heart to the task of developing them.

You can carry this idea into the newest frontier as well as into the most mundane job you are called upon to do. You can make it the greatest adventure of your life. With a modern application of this age-old thought, you can transform all of your duties into divine commands.

I find people living according to this "co-worker concept" all around the world. The Japanese believe that the spirit of crea-

tion is inherent in all living things. When they do their exquisite
flower arranging, their landscaping, their gardening, they believe they are helping the spirits (*kami*) to more fully express
themselves.

Or consider the new state of Israel. Here the building of a
nation is looked upon by many as the fulfillment of God's will,
in which man is a partner in prophecy. Elsewhere in the Middle
East the thought has always persisted that a task is better
done if the name of God is held in mind. Throughout India
and Ceylon, indeed throughout all of Asia, the sense of man's
relationship to divine destiny is vivid and real.

And, especially here in America, we find the idea growing.
American scientists and American youth are beginning to believe as never before that God has given us a universe to explore, to develop, to use, and to improve.

Can it be that He left poverty in the world so that we might
be challenged to overcome poverty? Did He leave pain and
suffering so that we might be inspired to bring comfort and
alleviate pain? What would life be like and what would be
life's growing edge if everything were magically accomplished
for us, if we did not have to employ our talents and our time
and our creativity in building that better life and that greater
world?

A legend says that God made men mortal so that in spite
of every other inequality we would have mortality in common
and recognize each other as sojourners and coworkers along
the way. This sense of partnership is the true catalyst and
equalizer of all mankind.

Tolstoy said, "I remember one day in early spring. I was
alone in the forest, lending my ear to its mysterious sounds.
I listened, and my thoughts went back to what for these many
years it always was busy with, the quest for God. . . . And
there arose in me glad aspirations towards life. Suddenly everything in me awoke and received meaning. 'Why do you look
farther?' a voice within me asked. 'He is here!' To acknowledge
God and to live are one and the same thing. God is what life
is. Well, then, live!"

That is it. That is the adventurer's call. Live! Live as though you were a co-worker with God in building a better world and in leaving your generation a little better than you found it. That is a life-changing idea waiting application by you and me.

"There is no Shangri-la," Stockdale said, "where all our wants are answered simply by wishing. Joy and success come out of the thoughts, the toils and triumphs of every individual who uses his God-given talents to help improve the life of man. That is how our country grew from a wilderness frontier and that is how a new standard of world civilization will be realized. Work, thought, creation, these give life its stimulus, its inspiration, and its deepest satisfaction."

Life-changing ideas can truly change your life!
Believe that God is good.
Practice the Golden Rule.
Be a co-worker together with God.
Make it an adventure!

14

The faith factor

Life is essentially a matter of faith, faith in ourselves, in others, and, most of all, faith in our relationship with the universe and its Creator. While we may have convincing arguments to justify many of our beliefs, it is faith that does the work, and faith is the great adventure.

In this search for a formula for the application of faith, people in all ages and in many religions have long agreed on a simple but thoughtful conclusion: *Do your best and leave the rest to God.*

This, they say, is faith, and we cannot help but agree with them. Of course, in looking back we often feel we might have done better than what we thought at the time was our best, but this is hypothetical. How do we know that if we had done better, the outcome would have been different? Had we done better we would no doubt have wished we had done better still. When we have truly and unequivocally done our best, faith should bring us consolation and not dismay.

We can better understand this when we consider the matter of faith and fate.

Some of the best adjusted people I know are fatalists. They have found the art of inner resignation without losing the art of inner compassion. I suppose they are "modified" fatalists, for they know that an individual *can* do something about

146

winning the battle against unseen forces. But it is at exactly this point that their fatalism works wonders for them, for they believe that when they have done the very best they can, when they have exhausted their ways and their will, then faith in God's way and God's will takes over. When in the final analysis faith has the power to absorb fate, that is truly a great conquest. Yes, some of the best adjusted and happiest people I know are fatalists of this kind; they do their best and leave the rest to God.

Something to Live by

The phrase, "Do your best and leave the rest to God," provides good words to live by.

A mother knows what they mean whenever she tucks her child into bed, says a prayer, and makes sure, as best she can, that the child is safe.

A doctor knows what the words imply whenever he has exhausted his ultimate skill and realizes that healing must come from a source higher and greater than himself.

A farmer knows what is meant by "doing his best and leaving the rest to God" when he has prepared and cultivated the land and planted the seed and fulfilled the conditions necessary for a hoped-for harvest.

A minister knows the power of the words when he has met the problems of his people with compassion and has given all that he can of himself in a specific cause.

Parents know the full import of the words when they have provided their children with the best they can and watch them go out into a "world of their own."

In short, everyone, whatever his resource or his responsibility, must eventually resolve his life into an adventure in faith based on the words, "Do your best and leave the rest to God."

"The Will of Allah"

I was in Beirut, Lebanon, when a ship ran aground in the Mediterranean, three miles south of Beirut Harbor. When

news of the disaster was flashed across the city, a mad rush
started to the shoreline near the little village of Ouzahi.

As my companion and I took a short cut we spied an aged
Lebanese standing in the doorway of his candy shop quietly
fingering a *masbaha*, a string of beads which Moslems toy
with and pray over and often use as a means of calming themselves down. We paused to ask this old man directions. Then,
as we hurried away, my companion called back, "Aren't you
coming?"

The storekeeper raised his eyes. "What is the hurry?" he
asked.

"The ship's going down!"

"Yes, yes," was the solemn reply. "It was the will of Allah."

Even as I wondered what the world would be like if we all
took such a philosophical view of things, my pace slowed and
I caught myself repeating his words, "The will of Allah."

I asked myself, "Is anything really beyond God's will?" For
Allah is, of course, the Arabic name for God. "Does anything
actually happen without His permission? The sparrow's fall,
the toppling of an empire, failures and successes in the inner
life or far off in outer space: where shall we say His will ends
and man's will begins?"

I have not resolved these imponderable questions, but often
now, when I find myself beating out my life against something seemingly inevitable, a vision comes to mind. I see the
mellow, bearded, sepia-colored storekeeper standing in the
doorway of his shop silently counting his beads as if they were
the precious heartbeats of eternal time, and I hear him say,
"The will of Allah."

As I recall, there was absolutely nothing my companion and
I did to help save the good ship *Champollion*. Twenty-six
people drowned. I do not know why they drowned and why
others were spared. I do know that those who were rescued
were hindered more than helped by our presence at the scene.
Oh, yes, we had a reward. A conversation piece. We could say,
"We were there when the *Champollion* broke apart. Some say
the captain mistook the airport beacon for a harbor light. . . ."

I had another reward: the will of Allah.

To Trust or Not to Trust

Faith is the factor. We must have faith in order to move confidently in this mysterious universe, our home. We must live closer to the source of life and truth, and even when we cannot understand, we must believe.

What is wrong with believing in God's will to such an extent that we try to see meaning in every circumstance, and that we feel ourselves part of the whole advancing process of life? Perhaps we cannot ever escape sorrow, and compassion we must surely share, but how about trusting God a bit more than we customarily do?

Can it be that sometimes, because of some deep, dark-seated pride, we ourselves want to play God and insist on having things go *our* way? Is it possible that we try to crowd God out of the picture simply because we want to crowd ourselves in? To trust or not to trust, that is the question.

When I see the non-Christian Asians and Indians sitting in their doorways or on the ancient curbs, calmly fanning themselves, fingering their rosaries, thinking whatever they are thinking, smiling I know not why, waiting for I know not what, I want to say to them, "Get excited about something! Worry about something! Light a fire under something! Time and the world are moving, don't just sit there!"

I watch them as they go to their temples with folded hands. Their thoughtful steps, their serene, enigmatical faces, their mellow yet proud attitude spur me to a thought. I say to myself, "No wonder there are no big industries here. No wonder we Americans must make the machines and build the cars and teach these people what progress means and even help feed their poor."

I go into the temples with them. I hear the gongs and smell the incense and feel the detached presence from the world of things, the presence that cannot be put into words, but which transforms existence into something higher than reality.

I worship with them. It is like worshiping with the deeply religious people of the Christian faith or any faith where men

and women respond in the presence of God. It is then that I
ask myself, "Is their sense of timeless living really a backward
step? Is it right for me to say to them, 'Get excited about something! Light a fire under something!'"

A sudden loneliness and longing take hold of me in the midst
of the worship and I feel that perhaps *I* have lost something
in my excited, hurried life, and that I have sacrificed something in my ambitious striving and my frenzy to "make good."
Maybe this something can be found again only by coming
down for a while from the ladder of self, for I have often been
humbled by the joy and peace of people who have far less
than I when it comes to this world's goods. I tell myself that
I ought to delegate more of my life to that Higher Power and
get a more balanced perspective on things. That is where I
must make it an adventure!

How about you?

The art of not getting upset means that we should literally
place into God's hands not only circumstances beyond our
control, but life itself as it has been given to us to live.

Faith is the factor. Faith urges us to remember that there
is a rhythm and a law in the universe, and that harmony with
this rhythm and this law is the secret of a successful, well-
adjusted life.

The distinguished, much-decorated naval commander, Ad-
miral Chester W. Nimitz, when asked if he had any secrets
to live by, said, "I have always made it a practice to worry
and be concerned only about those things over which I can
exercise control."

My friend, Dr. O. D. Foster, an adventurous Christian who
has had many a brush with death, told me, "I always have the
faith that God has an interest and a concern about my destiny."

The gentle Francis of Assisi, who became a saint, had a classic
prayer that said, "Teach me, O God, to bear with patience that
which cannot be changed, and help me to have the strength
to change that which can and should be changed."

In other words, stop trying to run life all by yourself. Recognize that a secret power, God, has a hand in making your world
go round. To believe this even when things are not always

going according to your wish, your will, or your schedule, that is *faith*, and that is making it an adventure.

Belief Makes the Difference

I know a man who is handicapped, but he believes that his condition has been more of an inducement to success than a detriment. He feels that difficulties make a man stronger than does ease, and that the only thing that can destroy a person is lack of faith. He believes in God more deeply than many a more fortunate man than he, and he has made his handicap his spiritual adventure. True, he has looked for healing and has quietly thought in terms of "miracles," but his true healing has been his inner experience.

It was he who introduced me to Carleton Everett Knox's lovely lines about "The God I Know."

> The God I know is a God close by,
> Not seated on a throne in a far-off sky,
> But is here on earth, reflected in trees,
> In mountains, in flowers, in sweet summer breeze;
> In ocean's grandeur, in plains' delight,
> In noontide glare, and the stillness of night;
> In children's prattle, in manhood's prime,
> Since the birth of worlds until the end of time.
> For the God I know with a thought that's free,
> Is the God of love, found in you and me.

Enter the Atheist

In one of my classes in comparative religions a young man got up to say, "I am an atheist."

He was not trying to shock anyone. He was not boasting. He was not trying to be smart. He had simply reached a point in his senior year at the university when he was convinced there was no rhyme or reason in the universe and that the much talked about concept of God was just that: talk, a figment of man's imagination.

This happened at the beginning of the school year. At the

close of the year I had a special recognition for the graduating seniors and among them was this young man. I said to him, "How do you feel about religion now? Have you arrived at any conclusions?"

He said, "I'm not an atheist any more. I've even joined the Episcopal church!"

"What happened?" I asked. "Who proved to you that there is a God?"

"No one proved it or disproved it," he said emphatically. "God is a *knowing* and I know. Belief in God is a matter of faith and I have the faith."

Perhaps I should have inquired how he arrived at this knowing and what changed his previous point of view, but he was reluctant to talk about his inner experience. Furthermore, I knew enough about students to know that they eventually work out their problems if given half a chance. And I knew enough about atheists to know that they really do not mean what they say when they deny God. By their denial of Him, they confess that there is Something that must be denied. By saying, "There is no God," they are themselves dealing in the faith factor, negatively to be sure, but in faith nonetheless, faith that God does *not* exist.

If anything at all exists so far as the nature of God is concerned, then, unless there is something greater than this anything, the anything itself is a god of some sort, or an ultimate or an absolute of some sort; and if there is something greater than the anything, no matter how unknown it may be, there is then an ultimate and absolute Something.

Belief in God *is* a knowing rather than a mere believing, but the faith factor is imminent in both knowledge and belief. As we said earlier, we may have ample proof and ample convincing arguments for the existence of God, but in the end it is faith that does the work, and faith is the great adventure.

Sankara Had a Prayer

A major prophet of Hinduism, Sankara, who lived in the eighth century, had a beautiful prayer. "O Lord," he prayed, "pardon my three sins. I have in contemplation clothed in form Thou who art formless; I have in praise described Thee who art ineffable; and in visiting temples I have often ignored Thine omnipresence."

Pascal Had a Theory

The seventeenth century scientist and philosopher, Blaise Pascal, who, though an intellectual genius, rejected knowledge in favor of faith, theorized that there are three kinds of people:

1. Those who serve God, having found Him.
2. Those who seek Him, not yet having found Him.
3. Those who live without seeking Him.

Each in his own category is exercising some sort of faith!

Paul Had a Definition

Paul spoke magnificently about the faith factor when, in his letter to the Hebrews, he said, "Now faith is the substance of things hoped for, the evidence of things not seen."

Mohammed Had a Parable

The prophet Mohammed made the people believe that he would call a mountain to him, and from the top of it would offer up his prayers. The people assembled. Mohammed called to the mountain again and again, and when the mountain stood silent and unmoved, Mohammed was not dismayed. He said, "If the mountain will not come to Mohammed, then Mohammed will go to the mountain." And he went and led his people to the summit where he prayed.

Schweitzer Had an Answer

Every rational faith, said Dr. Albert Schweitzer, has to make a choice. It must either accept religion as an ethical challenge or as a theology that explains the world. He believed that true Christianity chose the former as being of the higher value even though it meant turning away from a "logical, self-contained religion." Faith is the factor, he insisted, though men may scoff at it and though philosophers may reject it. Schweitzer contended that the faith in an ethical religion which appeared to some to be naïveté was, in reality, its profundity.

The Faith Factor

A graduate student in physics was having problems about religion. Like many young people whose old orthodoxies are exposed to liberal and scientific points of view, he found his parental faith badly shaken. He dropped around to see a minister who, after listening to the student's questions, said, "What you need to do is pray about this."

"Very well," said the student. "But how do I pray?"

The minister showed surprise. "How do you pray? You still believe in God, don't you?"

"I guess I do," mused the student, "but I am no longer sure what kind of a God I believe in."

The minister was so taken aback by this that he decided to preach a series of sermons on "The nature of God in the light of science and reason." He invited the student to attend, and the young man was there every Sunday for four Sundays. He took profuse notes and after the series was concluded the minister invited him to his study for a consultation.

"Well," said the clergyman, "how do you feel about God now?"

"To be honest," said the student, "I am more mixed up now than I was before."

Shortly thereafter, through a number of circumstances, the student began rooming in a home with an elderly woman who had no particular education and no persuasive arguments about religion or God. But her life of faith touched the student so deeply that he "found God" because of her.

That is how the transmission of faith has often been effected. When you try to put God into theological patterns or into a test tube or when you begin trying to define who and what God is and to defend Him and justify Him and prove Him, you may very likely be more mixed up than you were before.

God is like love. When you try to become completely logical and didactic about love you run into all sorts of difficulties. A wise old preacher once said, "Anyone who tries to explain love to his loved one on the basis of logical premises ought to be kicked off the premises."

Like love, God is a response in the human heart, an inner knowing beyond which there is nothing greater and within which there is nothing more personally meaningful.

When you trust your deepest instinct, who can say but that this is the prompting of faith? When an inner voice urges you to trust someone or to do something for someone or to follow your highest impulse, who can question that this is the monitor of faith making itself known and felt?

Faith is one's surest knowledge, though contrary to all logic. It is one's greatest call to good, though unproved and open to doubt. It is one's clearest guidance, though every rational sign may point another way. It is one's highest truth, though intellectual inquiry remains unable to prove it so.

Faith is the factor that sustains and motivates life.

Faith is the glorious risk that God is real.

Make it an adventure.

15

Lessons from religions

around the world

For some twenty years I have been visiting with people who live and worship differently than I do. As a Christian by tradition and a Protestant by birth, I have always had the feeling that other believers who were born in other cultures and in other faiths might also have found things to live by just as I had. Why this curiosity took the form of a life work, I do not know. I suppose there is first of all a personal quest in it. And now the more I talk to other people, the more I realize that my quest is their quest, too. The things I am looking for are exactly what others are looking for. The riddles I would like to solve, the responses to faith which I feel, the things I have found are the common property and concern of young and old all around the world.

What is the result of all this researching in the whirling world of faith? Let me in this chapter itemize some of my conclusions.

1. Man Is Religious by Nature

That is the first thing I have learned with a good deal of certainty. There is something within each individual which aspires to "know God." He might not state it just this way. He might not wish to use the term "God;" he may be disgruntled about the church and apprehensive, even suspicious, of "religious people;" but deep in the heart of everyone is an impulse to worship, to pray, to contemplate the nature of his relationship with cosmic reality, the universe, God, whatever name or reference he may wish to give it. I can attest to the truthfulness of St. Augustine's observation, "Thou hast made us in Thine image and our hearts are restless till they rest in Thee."

What does this conviction do to me? What can it do for you? For one thing, it provides a new orientation in the world. It assures us that we have something in common, something as real as life itself, something as profound as death, something as thrilling as the discovery of things unknown. We are adventurers together and we should take heart from this fact.

When I visualize the 3,000,000,000 people who inhabit this planet earth, when I remember that we are all made so very much alike, when I remind myself that over this immense family an ever-watchful, all-knowing Father presides, a Father to whom we have given many names and many faces, but who is the Creator of us all, I am at home in the universe.

2. Religions Have More in Common Than They Have in Conflict

Sometimes I feel that a recognition of this second point could form the basis of a new world order. For if we followed the deepest teachings of any one of the world's great religions we would have a world at peace.

How many major religions are there? The answer depends upon how you wish to define a "major religion." Some authorities claim there are eleven, some say seven. I settle for nine. These are: Zoroastrianism, Judaism, Hinduism, Buddhism, Taoism, Confucianism, Shintoism, Christianity, and Islam.

You may wish to add such religions as Sikhism, Jainism, the Baha'i faith, and many more. You may want to be even more specific and include some of the newer groups like Christian Science, Mormonism, Humanism; or extremely ancient ones like Osirism, Animism, Shamanism, and so on. But the nine I have chosen have stood the test of time and these, particularly, have more in common than they do in conflict.

Look at the world for a moment through these religions. Consider yourself a part of the great pageant of humanity. See how each of these major faiths rose out of a psychic or spiritual stream of man's everlasting quest for God and you will immediately feel a sense of unity and universality with your fellowmen. True, there are differences in beliefs and sometimes sharp cleavages in what is essential and what is nonessential, but remember there are differences in color, in culture, in food, in climate, in habitat, too, but we are all citizens of one world, just as we are all children of one God.

All of my nine religions believe in God. They are monotheistic, they believe in *one* God. It may seem that some of them believe in many gods, as Hinduism, for example; for in India you can find statues of a god of wisdom, a god of wealth, a god of mercy, and so on. Actually, these are not statues of gods; they are statues of the attributes of the one God.

It may be difficult for us to understand this, but remember that it is just as difficult for many non-Christians to understand our concept of the Trinity. Have you ever tried to explain the idea of three-gods-in-one to a non-Christian?

Some say that Buddhism does not believe in God at all, but this is only because the Buddha made no reference to a personal deity. He felt that God must ever remain unknowable. He also felt that "God" was used all too often as an escape from one's own responsibilities, but over and above all that the Buddha taught looms the idea of ultimate consciousness, an absolute principle able to understand human beings and, eventually, to be understood by them.

Not only do all of these nine great religions believe in God, but they all believe in man. They believe that man is God's highest and most noble creation. All have a high moral code. All believe in the sanctity of life. All, as we have seen in a previous chapter, advocate a Golden Rule. No religion states it quite as well as the Judaeo-Christian tradition, but all religions seeks to say that beside the Golden Rule, the greatest commission is to love God with one's whole being and to love one's neighbor as oneself.

I have gone among the major religions of the world and have talked to many of their leaders. I have lived among many of their people and there are numerous Judaeo-Christian cords of faith which bind the world together into one inseparable family. One of these cords is the Sermon on the Mount. There is not a religion which has failed to find the greatness in these remarkable words. Their simplicity, their sincerity, their ethical challenge, their inspiration are the creed and code of all religions.

Another cord of faith is represented in the Psalms, another in the Proverbs, and many in the writings of the prophets. Consider, for example, the remarkable words of Malachi when, in the second chapter of his book, he says, "Have we not all one Father? Hath not one God created us? Why do we deal treacherously every man against his brother, by profaning the covenant of our fathers?" All religions ask this question.

Or, think of the plea of Micah as recorded in the fourth chapter of the prophecy bearing his name, "And many nations shall come and say, Come, let us go up to the mountain of the Lord, and to the house of the God of Jacob and He will teach us of His ways, and we will walk in His paths . . . and they shall sit every man under his vine and under his fig tree; and none shall make them afraid . . . for all people will walk, every one in the name of his god, and we will walk in the name of the Lord our God forever and ever."

I shall never forget my visit with a Buddhist along the banks of the Ganges at Benares, India. He loved the Buddha and could quote at great length from Buddhist texts and Buddhist teachings. But when he had finished, he sat in deep reflection and, looking out across the sacred waters and beyond the swarms of worshipers who bathed and chanted and crowded along the shores, he said, "You know, sometimes I think there is nothing more that needs to be said about religion than was said by the prophet Micah: 'What doth the Lord require of thee, but to do justly, and to love mercy, and to walk humbly with thy God?'"

I asked him whether he knew that this had been Abraham Lincoln's favorite text. Yes, he knew that. He had been in America and he felt that if Americans and the people of India would walk together under that saying, they could change the world.

All religions also hold in common the revelation of great prophets. Most of them believe that God speaks to men through chosen ones. The prophets are the spokesmen, the mouthpieces of God. We ordinary mortals may well get a personal revelation along the way, but the world-changing, immortal pronouncements must come through specially prepared and divinely appointed messengers. Among these, no religion denies the greatness of the Christ.

All religions, or most of them at least, have their sacred writings which their messengers inspired. All have their ethical sayings, their revelations, their holy texts which they hold to be inviolable. All have some form of worship and ritual in which these sayings and these messengers and their God is worshiped. All have their sacraments and their ceremonies and most of them their mystical rites.

I have learned, too, that in common with the spiritual ideals held by the great religions of the world, all believe in life's continuity. Some, like the Christians, believe that we will live again; others, like the Hindus and the Buddhists, also believe that we have lived before.

It may be that this speculation on the "world beyond" may yet prove to be the one great factor of faith which will bring all men together into a family of believers. For here is the great mystery and here may be the great discovery, particularly in this present highly scientific age. What all religions believe— life's continuum, its immortality—what Christians believe Jesus demonstrated and what most people feel in their hearts to be true, may in the near future be proved by way of psychism or science. When that day comes we may face each other in a clearer light and join hands in a conquest of the many things which now keep us apart along this earthly way.

I could never understand why this matter of life after death or any phase of religion had to be talked about behind closed doors as if it were family gossip, or why it had to be hushed up as if someone had sinned or why it had to be argued about or monopolized or fought over, when, by the very fact of open exchange of knowledge, ideas, and experiences, everyone's faith would become richer and everyone's life would take on new and greater meaning. Religion, it has always seemed to me, is surely as universal as love or food, as vital as breathing, and as much a part of life as life itself.

3. All Religions Represent a Quest

Religion represents a process of search and discovery. There are certain truths which have been found to be incontrovertible and certain conclusions which are incontestable; but there are yet other truths and other conclusions still to be discovered. The exploration of faith is like the conquest of outer space; there are always worlds beyond worlds and mysteries beyond mysteries. When we are willing to admit this, we will have a workable basis for cooperation even though we may not always believe alike. All religions represent a quest.

I remember a visit to the Claretian Junior Seminary in Compton, California. In a day when teen-age crime dominated the news, I found more than 100 boys between the ages of 14 to 18 preparing for the priesthood. They rise at 5:45 a.m. and begin their day with prayer. They follow a hard-and-fast schedule which continues straight through each day until bedtime at 9:30, and which lasts for a period of twelve long disciplined years.

Of course, many of these boys drop out, but those who stay, believing that this is their vocation, reflect a great truth: the God-adventure can be the total adventure in life. This is true of all religions. I have found monks and nuns and dedicated individuals in all of the major faiths of the world. Theirs is a quest for meaning and dedication in life.

No one has all the answers, but everyone has some answers. You have undoubtedly reached some conclusions which have helped you in your spiritual quest and so have I. What we should do by rights is pool our discoveries.

It is unfortunate that in the field of faith we do not have the inter-exchange of ideas that we have in many other areas. In the sciences and in the arts, in industry and in human relations, in sports and even in the field of cookery, we have shared our recipes and our ideas. But too often in religion, the most vital and universal of life's experiences, we have continued to work behind closed doors.

For example, have you ever wondered what people think of when they pray? What do they concentrate on, what frame of mind are they in, what happens when they pray?

I have asked these questions of worshipers in many faiths.

One said, "I fix my mind on thankfulness. Gratitude for my blessings is the key to prayer."

Another told me, "I visualize God as the highest and greatest love imaginable and I see my life as part of that love.

"I kneel when I pray. I close my eyes and shut out all worldly thoughts. I think of God as a great spiritual Father who created all and who governs all. Then I listen for His voice. His voice comes to me in the form of thoughts and impressions. I actually talk to Him and He talks to me."

Others have confided in me:

"I put all my troubles and problems aside and begin by saying, 'God, I want only to worship Thee.' I keep repeating this until there is no other thought in my mind than this."

"I think of the beauty of nature. I can pray best out-of-doors where I feel the fellowship with God."

"I mentally enter a golden tunnel. God is at the far end in a dazzling light. I go further and further toward the light until my consciousness merges with His."

"I sit yoga fashion when I pray. I breath regularly and say, 'God is my light, God is my life.' I do not ask for anything or expect anything. I just fill myself with the thought that my life is God's life."

"I think of goodness and peace and try to fill my spirit with them."

"I visualize two chambers—one spaceless and eternal, the chamber of God, the Father. The other contains all created things and is ruled over by Christ. I walk through these chambers led by the power of the Holy Spirit. That is how I pray."

"When I pray I make my mind completely receptive to whatever God wants me to know."

"When I pray I mentally hear Jesus saying, 'Come unto me.'"

"Prayer for me is just being still and feeling God's presence."

All of these worshipers had found something; all were still seeking something.

The secret, of course, is to start with ourselves. Someone may intercede for you or pray for you, but no one can truly "find God" for you. It is an inner experience.

You must begin with yourself and develop the inward look.

You must take time for meditation and prayer.

Life is the laboratory. Life is the heart of faith. Life is the great adventure.

You must give God His minute. His ten minutes. His hour. There is no other way. There is no greater secret. *You* are the one who must begin. *You* are the person that matters. *You* in your own faith, whatever the faith may be, *you* are the person to whom God will reveal Himself if you but take time to worship Him.

Right now, if you close your eyes for a moment and think of God—no matter how vague your concept of Him may be— you have already begun an adventure in faith.

An American businessman said to me, "We should not entreat God or force God or beg of God. We should simply become aware in body, mind, and spirit that we are possessed by God fully and completely."

He said that when he first set aside a few moments for prayer in his office, his mind was clouded by a rush of thoughts having to do with business, appointments, and problems for the day. His biggest problem was to "keep God in focus." He soon learned that each time he brought his thoughts back to concentrate on the thought of God, the thought grew stronger. Each time he warded off worldly thoughts, God became clearer.

I have learned this from many religions around the world. "When you start thinking about the Lord, the Lord starts thinking about you," is the way a Moslem put it.

When the period of meditation or prayer is finished, God should remain as a lingering Presence.

When you open your eyes and look upon the world, you should do so with a new inner vision. You are not alone, say those who worship, you are never alone. God and you are one.

An instructor in yoga told me, "If the spiritual exercises leave you exhausted, you are not doing them correctly. They should leave you calm and refreshed."

That is also true of prayer. If your excursion into the "silence" leaves you disquieted or disturbed, you are not worshiping correctly. You have merely sought an escape. Worship and prayer are "finding God" and God is always goodness, peace, and strength.

The "quiet time" or period of meditation, wherever it is sincerely practiced, always develops a feeling of the authority of the moral in God. That is, the immoral becomes opposition to God. The better the worship, the better the man; and, conversely, the better the man, the better the worship.

It is an adventure, a quest.

A person may be moral without any specific religious discipline, but he cannot be religious without advancing in morality. Worship always leads beyond the moral. It persuades the worshiper to be critical of himself and to try to be a better person than he was before he worshiped.

Four Kinds of Worship

"There are four kinds of worship," a Hindu scholar told me. "There is questionable worship which is merely an outward form. There is deluded worship, which is autosuggestion. There is reasonable worship in which one feels he is in communion with a divine spirit. And then there is absolute worship in which one knows he is identical with the spirit of good, the spirit of life, the spirit of time and space, the spirit of God. Asking nothing, this kind of worship receives everything. Seeking nothing, it finds everything. Absolute worship is an awareness of one's complete unity with God."

That is the whole idea of the spiritual quest. There is nothing noble in being superior to other men. True nobility lies in being superior to your previous self, in finding some kind of "unity with God."

That, of course, is what all religions teach and believe. They insist that religion should give us a new standard for life. A God standard. They say you cannot take fifteen minutes a day for meditation without getting a new perspective on your place in the scheme of things.

True spirituality absolutely elevates a man. It absolutely takes the resentment out of life. It absolutely removes pride and egotism. It absolutely gives you a new sense of values, a new meaning about things, a new insight on how to meet and conquer your problems whatever the problems may be. It seems incredible that there should be a source of strength and help so near at hand and that so few of us will take a chance on it!

The Quest During Tragedy

A young mother whose only child was killed in a highway crash told me how she found strength to meet the lonely aftermath of the tragedy.

"I went to church," she said, "looking for I know not what. Comfort, I suppose. It isn't a custom with me to go to church on a weekday, but on the day after the funeral I went to our church. There is a cross on the communion table. I knelt down in our pew which is also something we do not do in our church, but I felt like kneeling.

"I looked at the cross. It had never been more than a symbol to me, but this time I thought of what the symbol meant. I saw Jesus walking to Calvary. I saw all that had happened to Him, and I felt that it had all happened to my little boy. I could hear him say, 'My God, why hast thou forsaken me?' I could hear my little boy's last cry, too.

"Something came over me. I cannot put it into words. The only way I can describe it is that I was believing with all my heart that God is good and that He was concerned about me, as He had been concerned about Jesus. All I wanted to do was worship.

"Something said to me, 'Bobby is all right. Bobby is safe. Bobby is with you even though he is gone. There is no dying even though death seems real.' I had been looking for meaning and understanding. Something said, 'Just believe.'

"When I came home my husband wanted to know what had happened to me, what had changed me. I had no explanation save to say that I had found something wonderfully good, and that I now felt myself a part of it."

What Is the Quest?

The spiritual quest is an awareness of and an identification with God in the life we live. If a person wishes to be strengthened for life's experiences, he must feel himself supported. This support is provided through the quest. The quest supplies the driving power with the help of which the individual becomes greater than himself, and through the practice of which his possibilities are unlimited. Whenever you seek, you have already found. This I have learned from religions around the world.

4. Religion As the Basis for a New World Order

Wherever I go I hear people talking about peace. As one man said, "Governments seem so determined to have peace, they are ready to fight to the death to prove it is peace they want!"

People are disturbed at the new philosophy which has grown up in our time, the philosophy that it is possible to have peace through power, even peace through fear, when it has always been the teaching of the prophets and of the Christ that men should have peace through love.

One thing seems clear: every approach to peace from cease-fire treaties to power politics has seemed to effect little more than an uneasy truce, and the threat of conflict continues to haunt mankind. Someone said recently that young people used to say, "*When* I grow up. . . . " Now they say, "*If* I grow up. . . ."

In all of this the voice of religion has been strangely silent as if it had no solution to offer and no suggestions to make. Buddhist countries have recently publicized the fact that they have never willfully engaged in war and that they have never perpetrated a war. Hinduism has until recently always been associated with a Gandhian type of non-resistance. The events in Goa changed that point of view. Islam and Judaism, of course, have been embroiled in many misunderstandings and tensions, particularly since the birth of the new state of Israel. Confucianism and Taoism, lost in the seething, restless waves of change on the Chinese mainland, seem to have no adequate voice to speak in behalf of peace. Zoroastrianism is numerically too small to make its influence felt in this pressing issue. Shintoism has not yet recovered from the betrayal of its Japanese military leaders. As for Christianity, it has been involved in struggles almost since the beginning of its history, and yet the symbol of its Leader has always been the Prince of Peace.

As was stated earlier, as far as the idealism of religion is concerned, it is emphatically on the side of love and peace. You could, as has been said, follow any one of the world's great religions and be led to a world where man lives peacefully with his fellowmen and all live peacefully with God. But this millennial state has never been reached and many people have resigned themselves to the belief that it never can be reached and we will have to learn to live with war.

Other people have other ideas. They point to the fact that men *are* learning to live together even though they live in troubled times. Surface manifestations may indicate little progress toward amity and brotherhood, but, it is insisted, there is a groundswell of understanding which with infinite patience and irresistible strength is quietly changing the world. They believe, and so do I, that religion will one day serve as the basis for a new world order.

This may not be religion in terms of denominationalism but,

rather, religion as a spiritual experience. The ecumenical movements, widespread and impressive, which are bringing men
together on a basis of polity and new theological understanding, are being superseded by a *spiritual* ecumenicity which
recognizes the Fatherhood of God among all men everywhere.

There are those who believe that when an individual has a
deeply spiritual experience, he is "at one" with his fellowman
who has also had such an experience, regardless of any sectarian
identification. This spiritual awareness is the catalytic agent in
man's adventure toward a world of peace.

This is the new approach and it deals with a more or less
imperceptive "conversion" which cuts across denominational
lines. In it the change is embedded in consciousness and its
awareness is not always shouted from the housetop. It is bringing all men together, men who have their loyalties in each of
the nine major religions, but who over and above these loyalties
realize that the brotherhood of man is greater than the sover-
eignty of sects.

I have stood in Gethsemani and on Calvary and in the Garden
of Joseph of Arimathea. I have paused at Gandhi's shrine. I
have walked at Sarnath where the Buddha preached his first
sermon. I have been at sacred spots such as the Wailing Wall,
revered by Jews, and the Dome of the Rock, revered by the
followers of Islam. My path has led into Shinto shrines and
to hallowed Confucian graves and into forbidden Zoroastrian
temples, and everywhere I have found the same heartbeat of
faith and the same dreams of peace. Men everywhere, regardless of culture or creed or color, would like to contribute to
this new world and not through any military campaign, but
through the quietude and conviction of their oneness with God.

Some groups, like the Baha'is and the Quakers and other
non-denominational movements, have already drawn up blue-
prints for a new world order built on spiritual faith, but none
can do it alone. It must be a cooperative effort and there must
arise somewhere, somehow, a leader of sufficient courage and
strength to make the goal articulate.

It is an adventure, perhaps the greatest adventure that ever
confronted humankind, more daring than the conquest of space

and requiring more courage than the conquering of disease.

This is what the world religious scene is like: there are today approximately 850,000,000 Christians. Of these, 500,000,000 are Roman Catholic, 220,000,000 are Protestants, and 130,000,000 are members of Eastern Orthodox Churches. There are some 450,000,000 members of the faith of Islam; some 330,000,000 Hindus; 400,000,000 Buddhists; 50,000,000 Shintoists; 12,000,-000 members in Judaism; 100,000 Zoroastrians; and perhaps 400,000,000 Taoists and Confucianists, most of them on the Chinese mainland. Besides all of these, there are approximately 400,000,000 people who have no denominational affiliation.

Whoever looks closely at these figures must realize that a new world order must have a spiritual basis and that this must be more than a mere phrase or a narrow sectarian approach. It must be built upon unity in diversity, a recognition of our common heritage as children of God, and most of all, upon an act of faith.

Though it may seem like an immensely big assignment, you and I have a share in it and are challenged to make it an adventure. For, as we have seen, the religions of the world are more alike than they are different. They all believe that man is religious by nature, that all faiths represent a quest, that there is one God and one Father of mankind, and that spiritual understanding must and will serve as the basis for a world order of brotherhood and lasting peace.

16

Spiritual healing:

fact or fancy?

There is something in our nature that longs to believe in miracles, and there is something in religion that seeks to satisfy that longing. Put these two convictions together and you have the answer to belief in spiritual healing.

"Miracles" are happening every day in the field of healing, if by miracles we mean cures which seem beyond the reach of known laws, beyond the highest skills of physicians, and above the most spectacular achievements associated with the healing arts. These miracles take place continually under the trained hands of surgeons no less than through the therapies and techniques of non-medical practitioners.

But what about "spiritual healing" of the kind associated with the power of prayer, the "laying on of hands," the act of faith? What about the accounts that are consistently being reported by the press?

In Baltimore, according to a United Press story, doctors at Johns Hopkins hospital told watchmaker Austin G. White that his wife was dying. It was explained that surgery would be the only way to halt his wife's internal bleeding but that she was so weak she probably would not survive the operation.

"I knew then that she was in the hands of God," Mr. White said. "I never was much of a churchman but when all hope is gone you turn to Him."

So White prayed and appealed to the public to pray, too. His story went out over the news wires, and all over America people began to pray. They prayed for a woman they had never seen, whom they did not know; prayed because one man had asked their help, the only help they could give. A schoolgirl in Chicago made daily trips to church. A woman in Cleveland pledged herself to morning and evening prayers. A steel worker in Pittsburgh asked St. Jude to intercede.

Meanwhile, the doctors operated. Mrs. White did not die. In fact, in a matter of days she was sitting up and White asked the United Press to express his thanks to the people who had prayed.

He said, "Their prayers brought a miracle. I don't know whether God built Johns Hopkins hospital, but He certainly was walking around out there last week."

Everywhere the Miracle and Everywhere the Hope

The White story can be duplicated in every state and in most hospitals across the nation. We may not be the most "religious" nation on earth, but you would have to look long and hard to find a people who seek miracles, who believe in miracles, and who expect miracles as ardently as we. A child caught in a drain pipe, a boy lost in the mountains, an airliner in distress, a mine disaster—scores of similar circumstances and "acts of God" evoke our prayers, our faith, our confidence that prayers can turn the tide. From the sickness of Pope Pius XII to the illness of Liz Taylor, waves of prayers have swept America and people of every conceivable denominational affiliation have implored God for His healing aid.

Believe what you will about it all, one thing seems provable. The collective thoughts and prayers of a people, positively held and earnestly united, generate a power to achieve their goal. What part "God" plays in this, I do not know, for men have made God in various images; but a metaphysical or divine force does seems to come into play where the proper conditions are

met. These proper conditions involve many factors, but most
important is the unquestioned unanimity of healers and patient
and all who are involved in the patient's life. This much, at
least, my research has indicated.

Sometimes It Is an Individual Matter

I recently met a man who had changed from a sickly, self-
pitying, complaining, neurotic bore to a friendly, community-
minded citizen by the simple process of reading and believing
an affirmation. The affirmation said:

> The Spirit of God is in me and there is no miracle that it can-
> not perform. I am the only one who controls its flow. I can
> shut it off or I can turn it on. To the exact degree that I be-
> lieve in this Power, I have this Power.

This man told me that all he did was believe what the
tract said and accept it as absolute truth. The tract led him to
the Bible, the Bible led him to God; God led him to new revelation and a miraculously changed life. He said to me, "Even
though I am forty-eight years old, I had never honestly put
faith into action until I started to believe what I had read."

No other person, apparently, figured in this character trans-
formation. No prayers were spoken for this healing "miracle."
He simply "turned on the Spirit of God and controlled the
flow!"

This, of course, leaves many questions unanswered. Why had
this not happened before? Why did the tract reach his hands
just when it did? What made him believe the words, and even
more significant, what made him act on the words and have
the sudden faith that "to the exact degree that I believe in this
Power, I have this Power?"

Metaphysicians and "truth students" answer these questions
by saying that "the fullness of time had dawned for this man."
It is as good an explanation as any, but it still leaves unanswered questions, especially the one which asks, "Why did the
fullness of time dawn for him and why does it seem never to
dawn for someone else?"

The same question might be asked of you as you read these lines. Why do they trigger you to action or leave you unchanged? Can it be that the "fullness of time" is a reality and that on God's timetable, so to speak, all of us are destined for some great life-changing experience?

Perhaps it can all best be answered by the phrase running through this book and running continually through our life: make it an adventure! And it may be that the person who is ready and willing to make *healing* an adventure is already on his way to healing!

Fact or Fancy?

It is terribly difficult to separate fact from fancy in spiritual healing, the reason being that sometimes we only think we are sick. We fancy we are sick, and then we fancy we are healed. At other times we are actually sick and we are actually healed.

A cynic once said of spiritual healing that it is a real cure for imaginary diseases and an imaginary cure for real diseases.

Be this as it may, you can prove for yourself in your own life that if you think health you will be healthier and if you think sickness you will be sicker.

If you have a wholesome, hopeful outlook on life, you will feel better than if you take a morbid, gloomy outlook on life.

There is a unity that must be maintained between the trinity of the individual—body, mind, and spirit—and where one of these units is in imbalance, all are in imbalance. You cannot dissipate physically without being affected mentally. You cannot be mentally disturbed without having the disturbance reflected in disease. You cannot be spiritually inharmonious without being in discord physically and mentally.

I have discovered in my own life that sometimes when I am mentally disturbed I am actually just physically tired. Occasionally when I feel that my spirit is estranged from God, it is simply a matter of having too much on my mind. Frequently when I think I am overworked, I am actually over-worried, and vice versa. I have never quite figured out what is fact and what is fancy!

One thing is surely true. You can have all the degrees in the world, including an M.D. and a D.D. and a Ph.D., but if you have never learned the spirit of the adventurous life, you are lost. Perhaps we had better say the *approach* to the "spiritually adventurous life" for it is this that works the miracles and, by a happy circumstance, it is not limited to any particular type of individual. Nor is it confined to any special group or any one religion or to any specific culture or race. It is a technique and an awareness, a response to life by what someone called the "Man Inside."

True healing is an adventure and whether it is fact or fancy makes little difference in the result which is achieved. Doctors have often told me that they wished they could inspire in their patients the faith and the "will to be well" which evangelistic healers inspire in their subjects. "Miracles" definitely require faith and believability.

You Are Not As Sick As You Think!

The above words greeted me when I walked into—of all places—a doctor's office. That was why I had come. I had heard about the sign and I wanted to see it for myself.

"Is this good business?" I asked the doctor.

"I think it is," he said, "especially if you believe as I do that a doctor's job is to treat the whole patient. One of the areas that needs treatment most of all is the patient's mental outlook."

"But is the slogan true?"

"In about eighty-five percent of the cases."

Most medical doctors agree. So do non-medical doctors and psychologists, analysts, and clinical consultants. The imagined disease may, of course, be fully as devastating as the real thing and the psychosomatic condition may be deep-seated, but if the patient has the will to be well, his battle is more than half won.

Your attitude, mental, physical, spiritual, is your best therapy and your adventurous will is the greatest power at your disposal. How far does the power extend? It used to extend to moods, then to functionary diseases. Now it includes certain organic diseases, and there are authorities who speculate that all ills may one day be traced to the *power of negative thought.*

How Powerful
Is the Power of the Spirit?

"God wants me to be well!" is a powerful affirmation. It has definitely changed lives.

So have other affirmations changed lives. You can try some of them for yourself and the proof will be found in what they do to *you.* Any case history may encourage you to try an affirmation, but the employment of one in your own life at your own point of need is where the most convincing evidence will be found. Prove for yourself whether the results are fact or fancy.

Want to try one for a cold? Yes, some people believe with all their heart and mind that colds can be overcome through affirmations. They tell me they can immunize themselves against the common cold by saying and holding to the thought that:

I do not believe in colds, weakness, or negativeness of any kind. I am strong, bold, fearless and free, and I am filled with the energy, vigor, and vitality of omnipresent, omnipotent life.

Some go even further. Not only do they claim to overcome pernicious colds, they insist they have conquered an even more stubborn and universal impediment: presbyopia, which means the deterioration of sight at the age of forty or thereabout. I have found people far past this age who use no glasses and who give credit to an affirmation firmly believed in and rigorously practiced:

I deny all belief in failing eyesight. My eyes are the eyes of Spirit, strong, youthful, clear-sighted, and perfect.

How about something even more "bizarre"? Take the matter of aching feet. Do you suppose spiritual healing can extend

even to podiatrics? Some spiritual healing enthusiasts insist
it can. They have an affirmation for such conditions, too, and
they confidently affirm:

> The harmonizing, healing, adjusting power of God now blesses
> my feet with strength and comfort, making them perfect.

One of my earliest research ventures in the field of healing
by way of affirmations took me to a woman who claimed she
had been healed of multiple sclerosis through the reading of a
poem! Would you believe it? The incredible thing is that several doctors I talked to about this case do believe it. Fact or
fancy? They are not quite sure, for they themselves do not
know the full extent of the healing power of the Spirit.

The poem which this bedridden young woman read and
which, she claims, effected her cure, was Unity's famous
Prayer of Faith which says:

> God is my help in every need,
> God does my every hunger feed;
> God walks beside me, guides my way
> Through every moment of the day.

> I now am wise, I now am true,
> Patient, kind, and loving too.
> All things I am, can do, and be
> Through Christ, the Truth that is in me.

> God is my health, I can't be sick;
> God is my strength, unfailing, quick;
> God is my all, I know no fear,
> Since God and love and Truth are here.

How Objective Dare We Be?

Most of the healing "miracles" I have observed, whether
they happened at Lourdes, at St. Ann de Beaupré, in Episcopal
healing services, at spiritual retreats, or in the tents of healing
evangelists, have left many questions unresolved and unanswered. I do not say that this makes them any less valid, for,

in many cases, particularly at Lourdes, "miracles" must be attested to by medical practitioners. But the fact remains that the entire riddle has never been conclusively solved.

For example, if an individual is sick because of a certain dissipation or overindulgence, what right has he to expect a healing without correcting the cause? If you tie a string around your finger tighter and tighter, the finger will eventually decay and die, and it is unreasonable to suppose that all the affirmations, prayers, and scripture texts will save the finger. You must be sufficiently adventurous to remove the string.

In cases of spiritual healing, however, the teaching is not always clear. God is asked to heal the individual without first changing the individual. Often miracles are sought and claimed without the necessary corrective disciplines which rightly relate to the rehabilitation of the total self.

Some spiritual healers, of course, emphasize this correlation and have done so since the beginning of time. They know that whoever lives in conflict with absolute principles and values which he knows he should live by and conform to, but does not, is bound to suffer.

There is another thing. In olden days suffering and sickness were looked upon as refining fires. It was said by religionists that these adversities helped men develop a more sympathetic consciousness, made them more tenderly inclined toward their fellowmen, and warned them of their obligations to themselves and society. Scripture glorified suffering, as when Job said, "Even though He slay me, yet will I trust Him," or when the Psalmist affirmed, "I know that thou in faithfulness hast afflicted me," or when the writer of Proverbs declared, "My son, despise not the chastening of the Lord, neither be weary of His correction."

But today, spiritual healers apparently are disinclined to put any heavenly sanction upon sickness and are also reluctant to say that God alone can do the healing. Most spectacular "faith healers" make it clear that they are "not opposed to doctors," and urge their patients to seek medical skill while still giving the impression of a kind of magical omnipotence.

Yes, there are many questions left unanswered, but the fact

remains that in the miracle of healing, as in the miracle of love, we apparently cannot be completely objective or reduce the experiences to natural laws. Wonderful things, it is said, take place when God is on our side, but think of what can happen when we are on the side of God!

Psychiatry and Religion

Because Sigmund Freud called religion a delusion and because many psychiatrists in their humanistic emphasis do not conform to religious orthodoxy, and also because quite a number of psychiatrists are agnostics, church people often look at psychiatry with veiled suspicion.

To these, the voice of psychiatrist Keith A. Yonge comes as a reassuring note that religion and psychiatry can indeed be compatible and can work together for the health and integration of modern man. Admitting that religion regards man as a divine being and that psychiatry views man from a scientific, naturalistic point of view, Dr. Yonge makes a significant observation.

"Where," he asks, "does the natural man end and the divine man begin? Nobody has been able to say. Take love for example. Try to separate the natural, protective care of parents for their children, which is seen also in animals . . . and separate them from what you might call spiritual love with its self-sacrificing devotion and mystical ecstasy, and you cannot separate them distinctly. Neither can you separate divine mind from spirit.

"Suppose," he goes on to say, "there isn't any clear division between the natural and the spiritual in man? Suppose the one is the extension of the other. Nowadays many psychiatrists and clergymen see it that way; they see man as both a natural being and a spiritual being, which are different extensions of the same thing. I say 'nowadays,' but actually the idea is as old as Hippocrates who lived about 400 years B.C. when men used to separate one disease from the other by calling one sacred and the others natural. Hippocrates said you could not separate them like that. He said *all* diseases were natural and that they followed natural laws, but he went on to explain that this did not mean that they were not divine. In fact, he believed quite definitely that they were all natural phenomena and, at the same time, all divine. He was simply pointing out that the laws of nature were also the laws of God."

All early religions had this secret. They believed that nature and God are one, and this is a point of view that modern man is coming around to once more. It has a bearing upon his quest for healing. He is beginning to recognize that everything in life is divine spirit and that this spirit has to have free flow in order to be utilized. It cannot be impinged by doubt, fear, guilt, or apprehension if an individual is to be truly *healed*.

Healing comes through the unquestioned faith that *God is life,* all life; that *God is good,* all good; and that therefore sickness and evil must flee as phantoms before this affirmation.

In her *Lessons in Truth,* Dr. H. Emilie Cady puts it this way, "No matter how sick or weak or inefficient you seem to be, take your eyes and thoughts off the *seeming,* and turn them within to the central fountain there, and say calmly, quietly, but with steadfast assurance: *This appearance of weakness is false: God, manifest as life, wisdom and power, is now flowing into my entire being and out through me to the external.* You do not change God's attitude toward you one iota, but you change your attitude toward Him. By thus affirming, you put yourself in harmony with divine law, which is always working toward your good and never toward your harm or punishment."

This is the heart of the matter. Spiritual healing demands this kind of faith whether it is done in the name of Jesus Christ, in the name of God, or in the name of Truth. The seeker for spiritual healing must be inwardly prepared to receive this healing unquestioningly. To him who does so receive it, it is fact; to him who does not it is fancy unless there is awakened within him the belief in healing even though he be not immediately healed.

The Great Physician

Jesus had a psychologically sound, spiritually reliable formula for conquering certain types of psychoses, neuroses, and personality disorders. He said, in effect, "Get rid of your guilt and you will be rid of your fear; get rid of your fear and you will be rid of your disease."

Like the best of psychiatrists and the best of ministers, Jesus did not preach to his patients or try to fit them into a mold. He utilized the raw material of the patient's life in his attempt at guidance. What He invariably did first was inspire faith in God and cause the individual to look upon himself as a total child of God. When the palsied man was brought to Him the first words were not spoken to his physical condition or to his bodily distress. Jesus said, "Son, thy *sins* be forgiven thee." When He healed the impotent man at the pool of Bethesda, He said, "Sin no more, lest a worse thing come upon thee."

To repeat, get rid of sin, get rid of the guilt, and you get rid of the fear. Get rid of the fear and you have opened the channel of physical healing. When the father of the epileptic boy said, "Master, if thou canst *do* anything. . . ." Jesus interrupted him and said, "If thou canst *believe!* All things are possible to him that *believeth.*"

I know people who have stood in healing lines and have not been healed. I know parents who have taken a sick child and driven many miles to shrines, to spiritual healers, to hallowed healing missions, and then returned as afflicted as they were before. But wherever faith was strengthened, the hope of healing was strengthened, too, and who is to say what miracle may yet happen to these who so earnestly sought and believed?

I know people who prayed consistently that a loved one might be spared and he was not. I have seen bitterness reflected in some of these cases, but I have also seen the miracle of faith bring comfort and meaning above and beyond the measure of "reason."

Fact or fancy? Only the heart can tell and only the questing liver knows what for him is true and what is false.

I wish there were a more definite conclusion that could be reached, but there is none. I wish one could winnow out the false from the true, the chaff from the wheat, the charlatan from the selfless servant of God, but I have no such presumption in choice or judgment. You can say, "By their fruits ye shall know them," but this does not tell the entire story. As far as I am concerned, the whole field of spiritual healing is exceedingly fluid and must still be extensively explored.

Where disease is the embodiment of thought, healing is more simple than where disease is the alteration of the human body and the malformation of the mind. I have yet to see a faith healer, no matter how adept, who will offer to work in our mental institutions or in the wards of the incurables where the public seldom goes and which half the world never sees.

I have seen healing miracles, but I have yet to see great miracles of healing of the kind that were recorded in Galilee.

Somehow I feel that behind great miracles must be the *life*, the life of God perfectly lived and expressed for one transfigured moment by both healer and healed. And sometimes it seems to me that this miracle is so very near to each of us that we may be much closer to the miraculous than we realize. So close, in fact, that we may be only a prayer away.

17

Your secret adventure

in faith

Here in America where every part and parcel of national life is measured statistically, we are told by way of the Gallup Poll that 98% of our people believe in God and that the remaining 2% are atheists or agnostics.

Twenty percent of those professing belief in God claim to have had a notable religious or "mystic" experience and, according to the poll, describe the nature of this as being in the form of visions, dreams, miracles or sudden conversion.

In the event that you have never been approached by a Gallup pollster, you can chart your own spiritual adventure with a series of specific questions, twenty in fact, which will provide you with an insight into the dimensions of your faith in your day-by-day world.

Question One:
Can I Put My Belief Into Words?

Ask yourself, for example, "*What* do I believe about God?"
It is not difficult to profess faith in God, particularly here in the laboratory of faith, America, but what kind of a God do you believe in? How do you visualize Him? How would you

explain your idea of God to someone from a laboratory of atheism?

Then ask yourself whether you can put your profession of faith into words. Do you have a creed you believe in? What spiritual principles do you live by, work by, stand by?

Then there are questions about your belief in life after death. Do you believe you have lived before, do you believe you will live again, do you believe in heaven and hell? Do you believe you will be reunited with those you love?

As a Christian, what do you believe about the person and mission of Christ? What about His miraculous birth, His miracles, His death, His resurrection?

It has not been proved that a vital religion must be articulate, and it is well known that faith to some individuals is so precious they are reluctant to talk about it. But for your own personal test, put your belief into words and get a measure of the faith you live by.

Question Two:
Do I Live as Though
What I Believe Is True?

Here is a good question, one that the Gallup Poll would hardly dare to ask!

It is one thing to profess a faith and quite another thing to practice it. For your own secret adventure, ask yourself, "How much of my faith is mere verbalization of the use of terms out of which the meaning has gone?"

William James once suggested that the average religious believer had a religion "made for him by others, communicated to him by tradition, determined to fixed forms by imitation, and retained by habit."

How about you? Do you admire religiously-directed people and applaud religiously-worded ideas without ever living these beliefs in your own life? Want to make it an adventure? Then check what you declare against what you demonstrate!

Question Three:
Does My Faith Meet My Need
In Time of Crisis?

Whenever I speak to groups in foreign countries I am invariably asked, "Isn't American religion dependent upon prosperity and an over-abundance of *things?*"

The implication is that our faith is construed in terms of our high standard of living and that we are religious only because of our fabulous way of life. Non-Christians want to know what Christians in America would be like in time of national crisis, insisting that it is easy to be hopeful and optimistic when we are riding the crest. The faith that matters, they say, is the kind that sees a man through "bad breaks" and that guides him "through the valleys."

How do you feel about this in terms of yourself and your own experiences? When you try to rate your faith, ask yourself whether it is a stabilizer in times of triumph *and* tragedy.

The pollsters said that persons who had a "religious experience"—the 20 percent—held stronger convictions than those whose belief rested upon other reasons.

What do you think?

Question Four:
Do I Have Special Stated Times
for Spiritual Development?

While faith cannot be compartmentalized and while religion should not be restricted to certain areas or special hours, people of great faith have always set aside stated times for meditation, prayer, and spiritual exercises.

I once asked a priest for the secret of success of Fulton Sheen. He said, "His strength and influence are generated in the silence." Martin Luther had the famous saying, "If I have six hours of work to do, I spend two of the hours in prayer."

You may not wish to go along with Luther in this ratio, preferring, perhaps, to follow the suggestion of Lin Yutang

who called his technique "the art of lying in bed." He advised
individuals to be slow in getting up in the morning, to lie in
bed adjusting their minds to the affairs and problems of the
coming day. A most convenient way to "pray," he thought.

A successful adventurer in faith said to me, "We cannot
remake our lives the way we remake our homes. We cannot
call in an expert to draw up the plans and then engage someone to do the work. Nor can we move out while this is going
on and then come back. We may get suggestions and advice,
but we must do the job ourselves, and to do it we must set
aside a special time for the doing.

I do not know how statistics are compiled by the Gallup
Poll or by other surveyors, so I cannot vouch for this report,
but one survey team told me that only one out of every five
thousand Americans takes fifteen minutes for daily spiritual
meditation.

What would be your answer to the question, "Do I have
special stated times for spiritual development?"

Question Five:
Is My Home Life Better
Because of My Religious Belief?

Signs along our highways say, "Church-going families are
happiest." "The family that prays together stays together."

While some insist this is merely religious propaganda, statistics prove that when Mom and Dad and the children attend
services in the church of their choice and are in spiritual agreement, home ties are strengthened.

Someone once said, "When a man 'gets religion' even his
dog and cat ought to notice an improvement."

Religious profession should build a happier family life and
you can rate your faith by asking yourself, "Does my attitude
in the home contribute to an atmosphere of affection, mutual
respect, and cheerfulness? Do I properly reflect the deep
convictions of the faith that is mine?"

Some theologians say that we are duty bound to love all
men, but that does not mean we must love them equally.

Nearest and dearest to each person, next to his love for God, should be those of his immediate family. In his home a person should exercise as perfectly as possible the four major moral virtues: prudence, justice, fortitude, and temperance.

What do you think?

Question Six:
Does My Faith Give Me
a Sense of Companionship,
Especially in Moments of Solitude?

A common criticism leveled at us Americans is that we are afraid to be alone. We are told that we do not want to know ourselves or analyze ourselves. We are accused of looking for continual means of escape. This, we are reminded, accounts for our frenzy for cars, entertainment, juke boxes, radio, and TV, and our insatiable lust for travel.

How about making it an adventure in solitude?

True faith should provide a feeling of "cosmic consciousness." That is to say, our religion should give us a sense of oneness with the universe and its Creator.

How do you rate in this respect?

A friend of mine, sightless for several years and one of the most serene and philosophical of men, said to me, "A person is never less alone than when he is with God."

Question Seven:
Does My Faith Give Me
a New Outlook on My Job
and a New Approach to My Work?

The old saying, "Work is worship," is, of course, a true corollary of faith.

Of what use is religion in the workaday world if it does not provide a usable philosophy for the man on the job?

You can get an appraisal of the vitality of your faith by the way in which you find your place in the world, how you fit yourself into that place, and how you devote yourself to it.

A man can make his choice. He can approach his work thankful that he *has* work and that he is able to work, or he can begrudge himself the opportunity.

He can emulate the successful man and thereby become more successful himself, or he can envy him and thereby become embittered.

He can do his best and have pride in himself, or he can do his worst and be ashamed of himself.

A man's point of view, his assumed attitudes, his thoughts, his manner of thinking—all these have a great deal to do with what a man believes and how sincerely he believes it.

Question Eight:
Does My Faith Give Me
a Sense of Security
in Meeting Life?

A well-known story about the early career of John Wesley tells of his fear during a storm on board ship. In the midst of his concern and fright, he suddenly heard singing. A group of Moravians were praising God.

Wesley asked them how they got this way. He was told, "If your faith cannot serve you during a storm, what is the good of it?"

To estimate whether yours is only a fair-weather-faith ask yourself how you react to storms whipped up by worry, fear, finances, social problems, and unlooked-for emergencies.

Does your faith give you a sense of security in meeting life?

Question Nine:
Has My Faith Ever Inspired Me
to Do a Good Deed Anonymously?

I know a man who has a technique he calls "anonymity." He is convinced that the most rewarding act is to give without thought of getting, to help without wanting help in return, and to reward others without looking for personal reward, not even the reward of being thanked.

Isaiah has an interesting observation, "If you bestow upon the hungry that which your soul desires, and satisfy the afflicted soul, then shall your light rise in darkness, and your obscurity be as the noonday."

Anonymity is the physical evidence of spiritual belief, and the true charitable act should be wholly selfless.

In your poll of what faith has done for you, ask yourself what it has done for others through you—anonymously.

Question Ten:
Does My Faith Command
My Deepest Loyalties?

Meister Eckhart, the mystic, used to say, "The eye with which I see God is the same eye with which He sees me."

That sounds like a great adventure! It means that our highest loyalty should be our recognition of our "oneness with God."

Of course, the mystics always had a way of talking mystically. One of them, St. Francis de Sales, said, "Remain either in God or close to God, without trying to do anything there, and without asking anything of Him, unless He urges it."

The mystics ask us what we honestly worship above everything else.

What is the "eye" with which we see ourselves? What is the "closeness" to which we wish to stay? It is all very well to say that we want God to command our highest loyalties no matter where they lead, but how do we react when they do not lead us where we think we ought to go?

How deep are your deepest loyalties?

Question Eleven:
Is My World Different
Because of My Faith?

If religion does not change our world, it very likely has not changed us very much.

When we walk through life with faith, when we have what is commonly called a "consciousness of the presence of God," our outlook on all life should be deepened and refined. A new drug called LSD-25 is said to inspire a super-conscious state. People who have taken LSD claim that life is never the same afterwards, for they have been admitted to a world in which God is marvelously at work. A flower looks as though it were unfolding with vigorous life, food has a strangely spiritual content, the heavens seem truly to be declaring "the glory of God." Some enthusiasts think this new drug should be used as a eucharist.

Be that as it may, we, too, should look beyond and within things in a new way if we profess faith in the creative power of the universe. We should see all life as God's life, all scenes as God's scenes, and even when such inexplicable events as war, terror, and death confront us, we should seek to find God's way in dealing with these incongruous circumstances in our not-yet-perfect world.

Question Twelve:
Does My Faith Make Me
Sympathetic with Other People
in Their Quest?

Albert Schweitzer said, "Impart as much of your faith as you can to those who walk the road of life with you, and accept as something precious that which comes back to you from them."

Such advice is a real challenge, for there has always been a tendency among all religions to aim at a kind of spiritual exclusiveness. Judge your faith by both its roots and its branches. That is to say, ask yourself if you are firmly grounded in your conviction and still have a sympathetic appreciation for the sincere convictions of other seekers.

A Talmudic legend says that in the City of God everyone will have spiritual *Lebensraum,* room to live. Everyone will have space and freedom to worship according to his belief in the midst of others who may be worshiping differently, and God shall be a God to each one over all.

Question Thirteen:
Does My Faith Give Me a Hopeful, Confident Outlook on Life?

While the world's religions may disagree about many things, they all insist that a true faith should give a person hope for tomorrow and confidence for today.

Perhaps it is too unrealistic for most of us to take literally the injunction "take no thought for the morrow," but the Christian, particularly, should be hopeful and confident for the days ahead. No other religion has so surrounded itself with promises for this life and the life beyond. No other prophet spoke as assuringly about God's guidance and protection as did the Christ. His favorite image of God was that of a loving Father and the central theme of His teaching was that this Father cared for His children.

Test-check your point of view to see whether your faith gives you a hopeful, confident outlook on life.

Question Fourteen:
Has My Faith Identified Me with a Spiritual Fellowship?

Students are continually asking me the inevitable question, "Should I belong to a church? To which church should I belong?"

I tell them that faith invariably compells a person to identify himself with a spiritual fellowship.

"I wouldn't live in a town without a church," is more than a cliché. It is the honest point of view of most Americans, even of those who never go to church. The truth of the matter is that even though you feel you may not need the church, perhaps the church needs you.

"To which church should I belong?" My research suggests that we should belong to the church of our birth until or unless we find one which better satisfies our spiritual needs. Before you leave your parental faith, ask yourself if you have thoroughly sounded out its deepest teachings and whether you have actually explored the faith that was "handed down" to you.

A good way to assess your religion is to estimate your degree of commitment to a spiritual fellowship.

Question Fifteen:
Does My Faith Provide a Sense
of Inner Security and Peace?

Many religions warn us that there is something wrong with our faith if life becomes too easy. They say that the cutting edge of faith is service to others and a concern and compassion for all mankind.

But these religions also insist that despite this sense of responsibility or because of it, faith should provide inner security and peace. It comes back to the old idea of doing one's best and leaving the rest to God.

The mystics contend that peace of mind and soul are realized only in connection with religious practices by which is meant discipline of both thought and deed. Modern religion is especially interested in providing techniques in this area. While some suggestions may smack of magic and provide an easy way out of social obligations, true faith requires work and involves activity in "God's concerns." Your religion works best where you work at your religion.

Take time to ask yourself, "Has my faith provided me with a sense of inner security and peace of heart and mind?"

Question Sixteen:
Does My Faith Inspire Me
to Observe the Sabbath?

Is Sunday truly significant because of your religious belief or is it merely a secular holiday?

The traditional sanctity of the Sabbath seems to be steadily slipping away. What part has your faith played in this shifting scene?

Recently a minister told me he expected to see the day when automation would invade the churches. Dial-a-Prayers (automatic recorded prayer machines) are already here. Recorded music is beginning to replace the organist and the choir. Experiments with drive-in services and taped sermons are being carried on. This cleric was of the opinion that churches might soon devote themselves to Wednesday evening services and turn Sunday over to outings, sports, and travel in which people would be urged to find God in the byways and highways and the great out-of-doors.

As of now, what does Sunday mean to you? How does your religion respond to the Sabbath—or how does the Sabbath respond to you?

Question Seventeen:
Does My Faith Make Me More Appreciative
of Life's Blessings and Experiences?

There is no such thing as a complaining Christian. The terms are contradictory, for the first attribute of the Christian should be an "attitude of gratitude."

If we love life in all its moods and not only when it is kind and good and generous to us, if we profess to believe that there is meaning and purpose in the universe, ingratitude and thanklessness should disappear. Paul said that through his religion he had learned to be content in every state.

One of the most remarkably grateful people our country has produced was a girl born blind, deaf, and dumb. She has become a symbol of courage, faith, and saintly gratitude. Helen Keller is considered by many to be one of our greatest Americans.

To adjudge your faith, ask yourself whether your religion makes you truly appreciative not only of life's blessings but in all of life's experiences.

Question Eighteen:
Has My Faith Ever Inspired Me
to Embark on a Spiritual Adventure?

All great religions insist that the person who professes a faith should be different from the person who makes no such profession. Jesus made the statement, "You have heard it said, 'Love your neighbor,' but I say to you, 'Love your enemies.'" Then He went on to suggest other distinctives which should be looked for in the "changed person." Turning the other cheek, walking the second mile, forgiving seven times seventy.

The implication in these challenges is that the spiritually-minded individual should "try the impossible." Every religion has its witnesses in the saints, and Christianity is particularly rich in this area. The saints are those who embark on an adventure of the spirit.

Faith implies a willingness to live by faith. It means making your most difficult problem your life adventure even though there is no absolute guarantee that you will win.

Question Nineteen:
Has My Faith Provided Me
with a Philosophy to Live by?

A philosophy is more than a moral code. It is a system of thought by which, in both easy and difficult days, your life is lived and your acts and attitudes are governed by a sense of purpose.

A philosophy is to a moral code what spirituality is to religion. Nearly everyone has a moral code based on this concept of what is right or wrong, good or bad; but a philosophy deals with the totality of life. It is the science that investigates the facts and principles of reality and the structure of human conduct and persuades you to see your life in relationship to all life.

To look squarely and honestly at yourself and to say, "This

is something I can control with the philosophy that is mine," to have the wisdom to admit that there may be circumstances beyond your control and to turn these over to a Power higher and greater than yourself; this is putting your belief to work in your life.

Question Twenty:
Does My Faith Supply Me with
the Courage to Make Good for Past Misdeeds?

One of the greatest tests of faith is to make restitution where restitution is due. It may also be one of the most difficult assignments. It may mean "eating crow," or "losing face," or "making a clean breast of it." But most religions insist on it and put it squarely up to the believer, "Are you willing not only to confess your misdeeds, but to make restitution for them?"

Many of the newer religious movements frankly say, "You cannot live your best as long as you have sins over which the grass has grown."

True faith compels a person to go all the way, to make up with his enemies, to pay up his bad debts, to give up his selfish grievances. An old philosopher once said, "I never get excited about anyone saying he is 'converted' until I see him return what he has misappropriated."

True religion is retroactive. When you find a faith to live by, you should, insofar as possible, redeem the past. This provides religion with its deepest therapeutic value, its "changed lives" concept, its "other worldliness."

To rate your faith, make a list of your unrequited obligations, the people you have offended, the wrongs you have left unrighted, the mistakes still left unredeemed.

There is one way to do it. In fact, there is one way to approach all of these twenty questions.

Make it an adventure!

18

The lure of the unknown

A fascinating area of the spiritual adventure is the lure of the unknown. It has always been a part of the realm of faith, but rarely has there been a time when so many normal people have had supranormal experiences as is the case today. Explorations in outer space have added to the thrill of the quest, and many persons believe that a new interpretation of religion will evolve as interplanetary travel becomes a reality. Fantastic theories will also be advanced before these discoveries are "stabilized."

We are living on the edge of expectation, spiritual expectation, when men are talking about a possible psychic breakthrough, by which is meant something revolutionary and sensational in the way of some "other world" demonstration, probably communication with discarnate entities via an electronic device or portraitures of spiritual beings by means of some ingenious photographic discovery. All the world, it seems, is waiting for a spiritual marvel to match the scientific marvels of our time.

Cosmonaut Titov, incidentally, decried belief in God because, he said, "I didn't see him when I was in orbit! Where is He?" The fact is that even though Titov did not see God, God may have seen Titov.

The Wish to Believe

I think many people have the wish to believe in the supernatural and when I say this I do not mean that there has not been bonafide supernatural phenomena. There have been many such evidences. But there have been more natural occurrences which have been "blown up" into supernatural occurrences because of the wish to believe that we are partners with the mysterious forces that guide and rule the universe. This has always been true, from shamanism down to the present.

Nor is this impulse to be derided. It was interest in magic that gave rise to medicine, interest in astrology that inspired astronomy, interest in alchemy that led to chemistry, interest in myths that developed into philosophy. When the new skills came, they did not automatically cancel out the old. The lure of the unknown still beckons us on, both forward and backward into time, and the wish to believe is deeply rooted in the human soul.

Fertile Is the Field

Yes, fertile is the field of paranormal experiences, for all of us have been objects of the strange buffetings of fate, or whatever it is that plays its simple tricks on us. For example, receiving the letter just when we wondered when we would hear, or meeting the person just when we were thinking of him, causing us to believe in such phrases as "Speak of the devil and here he comes," or "Speak of angels and you hear the flapping of their wings." Then there are the uncanny times when "You took the words right out of my mouth," or the moment when "You picked that right out of my mind," or "That tune you're whistling, I was just humming that to myself." Or the intriguing times when you are forced to say, "I have the strangest feeling that I have been here before or that I have gone through all this previously."

An engineer of reputation and accredited qualifications told me how he had suffered from arthritic rheumatism for years and had reached a point where he was confined to his bed. His wife had to wait on him constantly. Then he experienced a reverie. He saw himself in a previous life, centuries ago, and relived in his mind a sequence of that life when he was in a chariot race. There was an accident and he was struck in the back by a chariot wheel and saw himself lying groaning in pain in the dust of the arena. Suddenly he awoke from his reverie and, under the impact of the realization that his injury was but a traumatic aberration, he got up from his bed healed of his arthritic condition!

Because I never scoff at any of these accounts no matter how fantastic or bizarre they seem, I have learned a great deal and have won the confidence of many people who, for fear of ridicule, have withheld their stories from other confidants.

Sometimes Spiritualism

One evening after I had spoken on my research in the field of spiritualism, a father asked whether I would make arrangements with a spiritual medium so that his wife could have a "seance." He explained that ever since the suicidal death of their son, seventeen, his wife had been unable to reconcile herself to the fact that the soul of the boy was not in endless torment.

Said the father, "If my wife could just be assured that our boy has been forgiven for his act, I am sure that would be the greatest thing that could happen to her."

I explained to him that I hesitated to arrange for such a seance because of my reservations as to just what goes on in these sessions. There surely is bonafide evidence. I have seen it and heard it. But there is also an unmistakable margin for error, deception, and fraud, depending upon the character of the medium and many other circumstances. What if this grieving mother were to go to such a meeting and be disappointed or deceived?

Nonetheless, the mother did arrange for a seance and, unbeknown to me, went seeking communication with her son. Following her experience, I received a letter from her in which

she attested to the fact that her son appeared to her in ecto-
plasmic form in the seance room, that he identified himself
convincingly, and assured her of his well-being in the spirit
world. A more beautiful letter would have been hard to find,
and greater consolation would have been difficult to imagine
than that expressed in this mother's testimony.

Now, there are those who insist that this is the work of evil
spirits, the devil, or the machinations of the spiritualist himself.
However that may be, in this case a mother's life was re-united
to a sense of faith and, according to her husband's verification,
she found peace of mind which she had seemingly been unable
to discover through any other channel.

I would be the last to urge anyone to go to a spiritualistic
seance, but I would be among the first to say that the heart
of the Christian message is belief in life after death and that
all that true spiritualism purports to do is to verify life's continuum with evidences of communication.

You can make it an adventure either way: in faith, believing,
or in faith, searching. Which is the better way for you?

I do not need the sanction of proof for my faith in life after
death. Seeing is believing, but feeling is knowing—and I know
I have the feeling. But, as researcher Louis Anspacher once
said, "I do need the evidence that even now, in my subconscious self, I have a wonderland of power and conduits of
approach to another environment, different from and incon-
ceivably greater than the physical environment to which my
little, clever, conscious mind adapts me."

It has well been said that in every aspect of life, and particularly in the lure of the unknown, there is never a hope without a certain fear; and never a fear without a certain hope.

A Cleric's Point of View

The eminent Episcopalian bishop, Dr. Philips Brooks, gave
this advice to his congregation: "No doubt it is best for us now
that the unseen worlds should *be* unseen. It cultivates in us
that higher perception that we call faith, which is as truly
perception as is the sight of the eyes. But who can say that

the time will not come when, even to those who still live here upon the earth, the unseen worlds shall no longer be unseen?

"In all times there have been men who, at special moments, have seemed to see beyond the ordinary bounds of sense and with their eyes behold the forms of beings who belong not to the earth, but to the heavens. Who can say that some day, centuries away, when this old world shall be far older still and shall have been purified by vastly more of pain and labor, it may not be given to men to see those beings of other worlds who, even now, are around us and living and seeking the same righteousness we seek."

Great Is the Adventure!

Anyway you look at it, great is the adventure into the unknown! True, some people may not need it, may not want it, may not wish it or will it. But for those who suspect that their life is involved in more than the earthly pilgrimage of some three score years and ten, for those who feel the beating of immortality vivid and real in their souls when, for example, they view the wonders of nature, when they hear the beauty of music, when they respond to the deepest impulses of love, let them seek wherever they can to find whatever evidence will lead them deeper in their search.

Never before have so many people found the visible world so visible, the planets so accessible, space and time so conquerable, and God so near at hand.

Never have so many people been so impressed by the few who have the courage and the evidence to proclaim that the universe is not a mechanism, but an organism; not a theory, but a thought of God.

Great is the adventure!

Reincarnation Is Another Thing

Wherever I go these days I hear speculation about reincarnation. Speculation is what it seems like to me, for there is amazingly little laboratory data available in this field.

This idea that we have "lived before" is an age-old theory and, as we have seen in our chapter on world religions, it is a well-established fact that millions of people in Eastern non-Christian religions believe in it. The lure of it is enticing.

What *if* this life is an extension of a previous existence? What if this earthly sojourn *is* but the preparation for another round of mortal experience here on earth or on some other planet? Would these facts, if facts they be, make a difference in your present life? They would if you believed in them unquestioningly. And many people do believe in them.

I know elderly people who are so persuaded of the truth of reincarnation that they are studying music, art, and even languages, not for this life, but for the next! They fully expect to "be back."

It is said that reincarnation explains many mysteries, such as the cause of suffering, the meaning of purpose in life, the riddle of prodigies, and so on. All of these imponderables are, it is said, the result of a karmic law, the law of cause and effect. We have made our present destinies by lives we lived before; we are forging our future destinies by the life we are living now. Consciousness can be improved with each incarnation until it is eventually reunited with God-consciousness.

This is the final goal and purpose of life, to become "one with God" and Eastern religions say it is unfair to expect this state to be achieved in one single span of earthly life.

A man said to me, "I am a Christian and I do not say I believe in reincarnation, but there is no doubt that minds keep on being reborn in various bodies. Great musical and artistic minds keep on reappearing and improving with each generation. The mind of Edison, which worked on communication devices in his day, is very likely working on them again during this current time here on earth."

"Then," I said, "each generation should be an improvement over the previous one."

"Not necessarily each generation," he said, "but there are always *individuals* who are improvements over previous individuals."

"Then why don't we have someone greater than the Christ?"
I asked.

"Oh," he replied, "maybe there is such a one in the world,
but he has not yet revealed himself. Or a greater than Christ
will surely come. Even He, Himself, predicted that."

Other Christians will have other interpretations, but Christianity will eventually have to come to grips with the question
of reincarnation. The concept is gaining new converts continually. We can say we will not give it a thought or have
anything to do with it, but the shrinking world is bringing
all religions into closer communication. Hours away from India
and Asia in time and even closer to them as far as religious
thought is concerned, we are all being drawn together by the
lure of the unknown.

It has well been said, "Only after knowing the true goal of
life can one have a definite purpose; only after having a definite
purpose can one achieve calmness of mind; only after having
achieved calmness of mind can one begin to think clearly;
only after one has learned to think clearly can one achieve
knowledge." To remember this sequence is the beginning of
wisdom.

The Pace at Which We Move

A few short years ago hypnotism was considered little more
than a vaudevillian stunt. One of my earliest predictions was
that it would someday be recognized as a therapy. This came
to pass when the medical profession put its stamp of approval
upon the validity of hypnotism as a science dealing with the
unconscious mind.

Not more than two decades ago people scoffed at the idea
of television. The promise that someday pictures would be
whirled through space and come into homes through closed
doors and locked windows was considered fantastic. Today
they come into millions of homes—in color.

Less than ten years ago space ships and talk of trips to

distant stars were reserved for science-fiction and the fantasies of a modern Jules Verne. Today the highway to the moon has been charted and the blueprint to the planets has been composed.

These and other equally incredible marvels make modern man reappraise his scepticism of the miracles of faith with which the path of every living religion is strewn. We live in the midst of miracles. Life is the miracle. Thought is the miracle. Our place in this spinning universe is the miracle.

The pace at which we move makes it conceivable that within the lifetime of many of us, there *will* be a "spiritual breakthrough." We will hear about a new revelation, see ever greater miracles, and be drawn into a new environment in which the spirit of man will be recognized as the spirit of God at work in the world.

It was only yesterday that the term ESP was introduced, yet today almost everyone is familiar with extra-sensory perception, accepts its place in our social relations, and is willing to give consideration to the effect of this "psi" phenomenon in the personal life.

An ESP Interlude

Not long ago a four-year old farmboy was lost near the little town of Winthrop, Iowa. He had not been found when night came, and with the night came a blizzard of terrifying proportions. After two days of frustrating search by volunteer posses, a member of the Civil Aeronautics Patrol, whose plane had scoured the area, suggested that an ESP man be consulted. Why not telephone Mr. G. Croiset, the paragnost of Utrecht, Holland?

The parents agreed. The call was completed on the overseas telephone, and Dr. Croiset, who had never been in Iowa, transmitted the information that the boy would be found near an overpass three and one-half miles from the farm home in a grove of trees.

The advisement sent a stir of hope through the cold and

weary groups of searching men, for there was, indeed, an overpass corresponding to the mileage given. There was also the
grove of trees, but thorough searching in the snow did not reveal the boy.

Three days later the family telephoned Holland again. Dr.
Croiset said it still seemed to him that the boy had passed that
way, near the overpass, but he begged them to locate an
abandoned shack on a side road and proceed two hundred
meters southward from this. The boy, he felt, would be found
there.

Once more the uncanny perception of a man some 5000
miles away stirred the imagination of those who knew the
Iowa countryside, for there was, indeed, an abandoned shack
on a side road nearby. Again the area was searched, but without success.

Three weeks went by. Then I took a shirt belonging to the
little boy to the psychometrist, Peter Hurkos. He, too, had
never been near the Winthrop area, but when his hands
fingered the shirt and he got the missing boy's "vibrations,"
he launched into an uncanny description of both the boy
and the countryside.

Mr. Hurkos announced that the boy would be found in "a
small depression in the ground, like a very small ravine. The
child is lying there under the snow, face down. The child had
big eyes, pony hair. He is dead."

I asked about the exact location of the body, but this was
not forthcoming. The psychometrist did, however, indicate
that it would be discovered close to the house. This seemed
unlikely in view of the searching that had been going on so
intensely for so many days.

"When will he be found?" I asked.

"Within two weeks," was the reply.

Eleven days went by. It was now the Saturday before Easter.
A thorough and sudden thaw came to northeast Iowa and a
warm sun rapidly cleared the farm of its sagging drifts. A call
went out via the press and radio for volunteers willing to
cover the ground once more in a step-by-step search. In mid-
morning, the search ended abruptly. The body of the boy

was found less than 300 feet from the house. It was lying in
a depression in a field, in a kind of small ravine, face down.
Nearby were his tiny boots, mired in the soggy earth.

The Gospel of the Quest

The quest for understanding of the unknown forces of life
has become a kind of universal gospel. It knows no denominational lines, asks no prescribed creed, seeks no institutionalized
pattern, and wants only the earnest spirit of man as its credential for membership in this mystical fellowship.

It was probably destined, when man became man, that
his greatest rendezvous should be with the mystery of the
universe and that his search for affinity with the spirit of life
should be his mightiest driving force. It is extremely difficult
to be "scientific" about this or to validate all the data. It is
difficult to define God because it is so difficult to define ourselves. Who knows us as we really are? And to whom will we
actually reveal ourselves? Why, then, should not God also
remain a bit hidden? It is a quest, and we are called upon to
make it an adventure.

Every person creates an image of God in his own heart. This
is his most prized possession. How he creates this image differs
from individual to individual, but it is always interesting and
some aspect of the unknown is always present.

You cannot rob a man of his religious conviction. You cannot talk him out of it. You will have great diffculty persuading
him that he is wrong and that your concept of God is right.
Argument may only drive him deeper into a jealous protection
of the God he knows.

When people go to church they look for telltale signs that
God is as they wish or will Him to be. They listen for hints
that the unknown is as they believe the unknown to be.

To my mother, God was always Someone who struggled
against the world because my mother struggled against the
world. To my father, God was Someone who looked with a

touch of humor on the world and who had his moments of fun and enjoyment along the way because my father saw the humor and fun of life.

It is a quest. The quest is the great adventure, and there will always be the unknown to lure us on in this exciting cross-word puzzle kind of world in which we live.

We stand in good company when we are willing to explore the mysterious forces that play upon our lives, forces which may be trying to get through to us, urging us to live our best and be our best.

We are looking at God through cleaner windows than ever before. Science has cleaned them. Faith has made them brighter. The quest of man has even opened some windows of understanding to a purer light of God and a fresher flow of thought than we ever had before.

We are in good company. We may not, like the prophets, live in two worlds at once or be able as were the occultists to have one ear continually tuned to the whispers of the infinite, but we can, at least, speculate that there may be revealing glimpses given us as our adventuring spirit lifts a corner of the veil of the unknown and as our honest searching brings us face to face with new discoveries of the soul. We are not isolated strangers in this quest. We are links in a chain of tradition all around the world.

Make It an Adventure

And so, as we come to the end of this little journey together, we realize we cannot speak of "my religion" and "your religion" as if the elements in each were different. The elements are the same. We are the ones who are different, and who is to say who is higher or lower than another, or better or worse, or further advanced or less advanced in his quest?

We have not found many people on our excursion into the personal, the social, or the spiritual life who aspire to be saints, but we have found people everywhere who wish to live life richly, fully, confidently and who know by experience that man in his nature and destiny is frustrated if he is less than his best and that he is homeless without God.

These are the people who, like you and me, have found their little world within the great world, and to whom this little world has meaning and importance for their particular journey in space and time.

Life, we have discovered, is not always easy or simple. Our problems are not always solved with a pat phrase or by a feat of mental magic. There are times when we must square our shoulders and grit our teeth and pray unceasingly, and every honest and sensitive person knows this to be true.

Prayers are not always answered as we wish they might be or in the way we feel they ought to be, but they are always answered. They are answered in ways that unfold with time and in that restoring hour the infinite wisdom behind the unfoldment often fills us with awe and causes us to see life in a new perspective.

It is often said, "No man has God in his hip pocket, but every man has God in his heart." You have God in your heart if in the face of life's situations you are able to say, "Nothing happens without purpose, and what is happening to me is part of my life's adventure. I take God with me into this experience." If you can hold to thoughts of this kind and live them in accordance with your highest ideal, you will find a resource and a compulsion never before known.

Always look for a greater good than the superficial good. That is the way life seems to work. That is how God works. He always takes the long view. He appears always to be intent on working toward eternal values. He is determined to reveal Himself in many ways, in many extraordinary places, and in many faiths, having a preference only for the believing heart. Always found where men will dare to find Him, and ever understood most perfectly through selfless love, He is, it seems, constantly whispering to us the magical, challenging, life-changing words, *"Make it an adventure!"*

About the Author

Marcus Bach has since youth been drawn to the knowledge of people as they worship; as a scholar and as a writer, his religious inquiry is characterized by sympathy with the believer in whom faith is embodied. He is presently a professor in the School of Religion of the State University of Iowa, devoting much of his time to research and travel abroad in the interest of inter-religious and inter-cultural activity. A frequent companion is his wife, Lorena, whose camera has recorded the memorable scenes and encounters of travels that have taken them throughout Asia and the Orient, meeting—on grounds of friendship—peoples of every faith.

Dr. Bach is the author of fifteen books, twenty plays, and numerous articles which have appeared in *Coronet, Reader's Digest, Christian Herald, The American Weekly* and many other magazines. Prentice-Hall has recently published Dr. Bach's *The Unity Way Of Life,* a definitive work on the Unity School of Christianity.